SYLVIA KRISTEL ~~~~~~~~~~~~~~~~~~~~~~
age of 17 she started ~~~~~~~~~~~
competition in 1973. Her cinema career was launched in 1974
by the phenomenal worldwide success of *Emmanuelle*. Having
won her fight against drugs, alcohol and cancer she now works
as an actress and an artist. She lives in Amsterdam.

From the reviews of *Undressing Emmanuelle*:

'An elegantly written book. The prose is simple, evocative and
highly readable. I found myself wishing that our home-grown
celebrities would write books full of ideas and feelings, not
glossy magazine therapy-speak. A few of her highly stylised
sentences tell far more about the whys and wherefores of
exposure and fame than all the trash clogging the bestseller
lists of late'   BELLE DE JOUR, *The Times*

'This is a poignant autobiography. Her story is gripping'
                                           Sunday Times

'For a sharp lesson in what it is to be the object of men's desire,
Undressing Emmanuelle is a darkly discomforting read. There's
no bitterness or regret ... this is the examined life'   *Observer*

'A remarkable memoir. A series of impressionistic snapshots,
delivered in austere, melancholic prose, it is quite unlike other
show-biz memoirs and its candour is raw. Sylvia is a cult icon,
she loosened our inhibitions. But the price was high'
                                           Gloss magazine

'A brave book, written with rare self-awareness'
                                    Sunday Business Post

Undressing Emmanuelle

A Memoir

SYLVIA KRISTEL

with JEAN ARCELIN

Translated from the French by
POLLY McLEAN

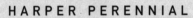

HARPER PERENNIAL

London, New York, Toronto, Sydney and New Delhi

Harper Perennial
An imprint of HarperCollins*Publishers*
77–85 Fulham Palace Road, Hammersmith
London W6 8JB

www.harperperennial.co.uk
Visit our authors' blog at www.fifthestate.co.uk

This edition published by Harper Perennial 2008
1

First published in Great Britain by Fourth Estate in 2007

A catalogue record for this book is
available from the British Library

ISBN 978-0-00-725696-9

Set in Minion by
Rowland Phototypesetting Ltd, Bury St Edmunds, Suffolk

Printed and bound in Great Britain by Clays Ltd, St Ives plc

Mixed Sources
Product group from well-managed
forests and other controlled sources
www.fsc.org   Cert no. SW-COC-1806
© 1996 Forest Stewardship Council
FSC

FSC is a non-profit international organisation established to promote the
responsible management of the world's forests. Products carrying the FSC
label are independently certified to assure consumers that they come
from forests that are managed to meet the social, economic and
ecological needs of present and future generations.

Find out more about HarperCollins and the environment at
www.harpercollins.co.uk/green

For Arthur

LIST OF ILLUSTRATIONS

Hôtel du Commerce (Private Collection)
Grandmother Kristel (Private Collection)
Uncle Hans (Private Collection)
Aunt Mary (Private Collection)
Reading *Donald Duck* (Private Collection)
Parents (Private Collection)
Mrs Kristel (Private Collection)
Miss TV Europe Competion (Getty Images, Ian
    Showell/Stringer)
Hugo Claus (Paul Huf/MAI)
From *Emmanuelle* (Getty Images/J. Cuinieres)
Jeanne Colletin (The Kobal Collection)
Marika Green (The Kobal Collection)
Sylvia Kristel (Corbis/ Francis Giacobetti)
Cannes Film Festival (AP/Empics)
Ian McShane (Corbis/Christian Simonpietri)
Sylvia Kristel (Corbis/Christian Simonpietri)
Gérard Depardieu (Corbis/Christian Simonpietri)
Eric Brown (The Kobal Collection)
Nicholas Clay (The Kobal Collection)
Sylvia Kristel (Corbis/Micheline Pelletier/Sygma)
Sylvia Kristel (Corbis/Micheline Pelletier)

Freddy de Vree (Private Collection)
Karlovy Vary Film Festival (Private Collection)
Arthur Claus (Erwin Olaf)

1

Amsterdam, 2005

Bessel Kok is a major businessman. It shows: he has presence, composure, style and a keen eye. He's a chess fanatic like my father, and a connoisseur of fine flesh and lovely women. His wife is young and ravishing, he has the pot belly of a gourmand, and his dream is to become President of the World Chess Federation.

He is also generous and – as luck would have it – a nostalgic fan and kind patron of little old me! I met him a few years ago at a smart dinner after a private view. He kindly invited me to the Karlovy Vary Film Festival in the Czech Republic, of which he was a sponsor. Bessel has become a thoughtful and protective friend.

This summer he offered to subsidise me.

'Why?'

'I will provide you with financial support for a few months, so you can devote yourself to your own project.'

'What kind of project?'

'A book.'

'A book?'

'The story of an ageing Dutchwoman, a former goddess of love, in fragile health and living in a tiny apartment ...' He laughed, adding: 'Give it some thought ...'

*

The sun was shining brightly on the Amsterdam canals, and life was cutting me some slack. My mind roamed freely in my convalescing body – I had time to live, to think. My pale skin soaked up the sun, turning more golden by the day and slowly showing up a scar on my left arm. Four white spots came gradually into relief, each smaller than the last.

'Give it some thought ...' Bessel's words kept running through my mind, refusing to fade.

I couldn't take my eyes off this scar of mine. So old. Forgotten. Four spots, like a secret code, the code of my childhood, of my life perhaps. A code I had never tested.

But now I had to; it was time.

I phoned Bessel in the middle of that hot summer and announced: 'I'm going to test the code.'

'What?'

'I've been frightened that I'd forgotten everything, on purpose or because I had to, but now it's all coming back, the words are on the tip of my tongue ...'

'I can't understand what you're saying.'

'I accept your support, Bessel! I'm ready to do the book.'

2

The last train has screeched noisily into Utrecht station, as it does every evening just after nine. Daytime was over hours ago, but night arrives only with this silence. A brutal cold snap started today.

'Winter is here, that's for sure!' declared a customer in the overheated hotel restaurant.

Utrecht station is enormous, the biggest in Holland, a great entangled fork leading to a huge, well-ordered platform. Travellers arrive here from all countries, for a day or a month, for the cattle market, the trade fairs, the hopes and encounters of big city life.

I walk slowly down the main staircase, the floorboards creaking despite the lightness of my tread. I am trying not to make any noise, in case the hotel is full – although the lights in the lobby are off. There's only that red light seeping in through the bay windows, lending a glow to each piece of furniture, each line, to the Chinese vase standing on the reception counter. This red light blinks on and off, banishing the night-time dark. In the hotel the dark is never black, it's purple.

The show is scheduled for ten o'clock. I cross the empty restaurant; the customers must have eaten early on account of the sudden cold. I walk towards the counter. It's the end of the week and the customers have left, tired.

I'm disappointed. I enjoy doing my little show. Usually the two of us do it together, it's better that way – we smile and protect each other. We always use the same song, 'Only You' by the Platters. I get on my bicycle and pedal around the bar, turning in the wide aisle. I fix each customer with a perfectly neutral smile, neither happy nor sad. I stretch out one leg, then the other. My skirt flips back over the saddle and I turn my head slowly from side to side, trying to make the curls of my short hair flutter. Marianne is behind me on the rack, waving. I meet the amused eyes of the customers without reading them. I check that everyone is happy. The recipe usually takes – they laugh out loud, encouraging me and calling out:

'Bravo, Sylvia! Do it again, both legs together this time!'

That's how it usually turns out, but not tonight. I am alone and I won't be doing a show for anyone. I decide to go back up to my room.

The lounge door opens, letting in a patch of bright light. I jump.

'Ah, you're here, Sylvia! You came. Is it only me? Come over here, Peter! Sylvia's going to do her show, just for us.'

I nod slowly, minimally. I can't refuse, can't say no to 'Uncle' Hans. I'm already wearing my performance outfit – the short wool skirt and a slightly faded pink T-shirt matched to my tights.

Peter is still wearing his apron. He's the sous-chef. He has a red, puffy face and large, deep-set, glittering eyes. 'Uncle' Hans always wears the same grey suit, unironed and too short, revealing spotless white socks. His face is round. His hair is greasy and plastered back. I can't tell the length of 'Uncle' Hans's hair. Is it long, under all the Brylcreem? As long as the hair concealed in severe buns which in the rooms at night cascades free and soft right down the backs of the women I sometimes glimpse?

'Come on then! Start! We've no time to lose, sweetheart!'

'Uncle' Hans turns on a table lamp so he can see me better. I get on my bike and go round once in their silence, I don't want any music. I stretch out a leg, not looking at them. I can feel their gaze. Settled on my body like a boil. It bothers me and makes me feel tired but I carry on, neither sad nor happy, I will not stop. I twirl around, I'm an acrobat, an agile cat, a beautiful lady. I pedal around the bar. 'Uncle' Hans puts out a hand each time I pass, trying to catch me as if I were a fairground attraction. I skid a little but regain control. One more and I'll stop, I've decided. That will be it for tonight.

'Uncle' Hans has stood up. And Peter. They're suddenly in front of me, blocking my circular route. They wedge my front wheel with their feet, grab my shoulders and put a hand over my mouth. I don't cry out. I knew it. Peter pulls my hands behind my back, takes a forgotten napkin from a table and ties them together, pulling hard, wanting me to wince but I won't. I stand motionless, waiting. I want to see 'Uncle' Hans's hair come loose, to feel his sticky hands soaked with fear. Let him sweat his desire over me, exposing himself as no one knows him. I want the boil to burst. I'm waiting.

'Uncle' Hans sticks out his thick, blotchy, pinky-brown tongue, waggling it like a hissing snake. He takes hold of my face – smaller than his hands – tilts it, and leans over so that his tongue can reach every part of my skin. He is slobbering, licking me slowly from neck to temple, from bottom to top, then starting again. His tongue is a thick, hot body, with a hard, pushing tip, so close but so foreign, so unknown. I don't move. I leave my hands knotted in the napkin, leave my face to be smeared with his saliva, let him do it.

'What's going on here?' shrieks Aunt Alice as she comes into the lounge.

'Nothing, nothing!' replies 'Uncle' Hans. 'We're playing with Sylvia!'

Aunt Alice comes closer, slender, quick and unafraid. She slams on light switches as she comes, making the bar as bright as daylight, then raises her voice.

'Sylvia, go straight back up to your room. You need to take care of your sister, she's not well. Quick now, it's late!'

I turn towards her, pulling with all my strength on the napkin still binding my hands. 'Uncle' Hans has stood up again and is leaving the room without a word, head bent. Peter follows him. Aunt Alice watches them go, mute, then sees the napkin fall to my feet. She hides her head in her hands with a great groaning sigh and repeats, her voice softer and slower: 'What's going on? . . .'

I am out of there.

I was nine years old. It was in my parents' hotel, where I grew up – the Commerce Hotel, Station Square, Utrecht. That was the chaos of my young life.

3

'Uncle' Hans is the manager of the hotel, which belongs to my paternal grandmother. The whole family lives or works here – my parents, my aunts Alice and Mary, my younger sister Marianne and the baby, my brother Nicolas.

The hotel boasts no stars but it is rather elegant, with its high ceilings, Persian carpets and art nouveau style.

'Uncle' Hans is appreciated for his rigour. He is steadfast, hardworking and clean, his nails perfectly rounded from frequent filing. He's the right-hand man, he opens and closes the hotel with the clockwork regularity of the station trains. 'Uncle' Hans has that inhuman ability to repeat impeccably the same mechanical actions day after day. His face betrays neither fatigue nor pain, just a slight smile. He intrigues me. He must be a robot, resembling a man without quite having the right expression, hiding under his smooth mask and shiny head a lifeless body, activated by strings and held together by steel rods and tightly fastened screws rather than blood and tears.

'Uncle' Hans is not an uncle but the head employee of the hotel. He owes his nickname to the trust my parents have placed in him, to his daily presence, and to the calm and protective impression he makes. It was my mother who first called him that. With the name she gave 'Uncle' Hans a stake in our family, hoping to encourage that solitary man to attach himself – to us, our good fortune, and our hotel.

'Uncle' Hans does not like me. I am the boss's daughter. His secret rival, an idle girl sprouting up before his very eyes with my lazy blossoming charm, the kid constantly under his feet, a growing obstacle, an unformed body arousing his desire.

I often eat with him and the sous-chef in the kitchen. I am already making my preferences clear, gently but firmly. I don't like onions, carrots or mustard, those adult items I'm supposed to force down my throat 'like a big girl', as he says. He likes to watch me grimace as I chew. The mustard pot is huge, family-size. It goes from table to table acquiring layers of congealed mustard on its rim, some browner than others, scored by marks where the spoon has lain. Leftovers. I don't want any mustard.

One refusal too many and 'Uncle' Hans's eyes go all red. He grabs my slender neck and squeezes it until my body goes rigid, then shoves my face into the pot.

When I've had enough to eat I push my plate towards the middle of the table with infinite slowness, looking elsewhere. I take advantage of any distractions to secretly push the plate as far away from me as possible.

'Uncle' Hans catches me at it, and stabs his fork into my arm. Hard. I scream and run to my room. The pain is intense. The blood is seeping through, making four red spots on my arm. I rub them as you scrub a stain, but it doesn't make any difference.

I hide the wound by crossing my arms: my first pose.

I tell my mother how 'Uncle' Hans forces me to finish disgusting plates of food. She replies that I have to do whatever 'Uncle' Hans tells me, it's for my own good.

I hit on a different strategy. I decide to spend any scraps of money I earn from serving or making beds in the chip shop next door. The chips are fat, greasy and delicious; they crunch and melt in my mouth as I savour their soft hearts, alone or with my sister Marianne.

We behave like starving orphans, and the kind owner gives us extra large portions. We are free, happy and sated.

When my skin turns brown in the summer, the four spots from the fork are reborn – one at a time, in a neat little row, from the most distinct to the faintest.

4

Aunt Alice told my mother all about the scene she'd interrupted in the bar: my hands still bound, the blushing discomfort of 'Uncle' Hans, his tousled hair, the way he left, stooped and staggering, looking such a hypocrite. My mother told my father.

'Uncle' Hans was dismissed the following day, with no explanation other than my mother's shattered and contemptuous gaze and the rage written all over my father's closed face.

My mother didn't want to know the details, she didn't ask me a thing. She doesn't want any trouble. She would rather sweep away evil as she does dirt – straightforward and effective.

My mother will remain shaken for a long time, thinking deeply about the roots of vice and men's ability to conceal it, to cover evil with a pleasant mask. Can good also contain evil? My mother's simple, two-tone world was quaking, the black and white blending to create new shades, new shadows.

I watch Hans leaving. I've triumphed over the robot. He is deathly pale, demolished, seemingly finished. For a moment, as the door slams behind him and the freezing air floods in, I feel a tinge of regret. Is the sentence too harsh, more than I'm worth?

5

The two nymphets are rosy-cheeked, and go topless all year round. They don't wear dresses, just a big sheet over one shoulder. Their hair hangs down in thick coils. They look a little sad, not yet smiling. I try to catch their eyes but never can. I watch them through the window of room 21, in the eaves of the hotel, where my sister and I sleep most of the time.

The nymphs reign like Greek statues on either side of the station forecourt. On the left is the source of the red light that gives the area's nights their bright, intermittent glow: an enormous Coca-Cola sign. I love the elegant writing with its upstrokes and downstrokes, and the funny name that rings out like a greeting in an exotic language. The light is intense and streams right into the hotel. It also tints the noses and breasts of my nymphs, making them twinkle.

I sometimes stretch my hand dreamily out of the window, watching my arm flush and fade. I am a station nymph, an angel ready to depart, a little girl on a journey. About to fly out of the window like a bird. I watch my flesh become flooded with the soft light, turning my arm, opening my hand then shutting it again. I do a finger-puppet show under the Coca-Cola spotlights and the gaze of my nymphs.

It's a funny kind of home town, Utrecht: a puritanical, grey, swarming business hub whose visitors are welcomed by two naked women and a huge red neon sign.

The door to my room opens, slowly. My mother pokes her head round it and is astonished to see me at the window in the middle of the night.

'You're not sleeping?'

'No.'

'And your sister?'

'Marianne always sleeps well.'

'The hotel is full. Wake your sister and take her to room 22, I've just let this one to a good customer.'

Room 22 is not a room but a cubbyhole, with a skylight in the ceiling and a single bed. When the hotel is full we spend the night there. I pick up Marianne's hot, limp body, telling her that it's me and there's nothing to worry about. I carry her upstairs while my mother tidies the room quick as a flash, and calls downstairs to the customer in her late-night auctioneer's voice.

The bed in 22 is narrow and cold. The customer in 21 will enjoy slipping into the warmth left by my sister, and fall asleep easily. Not me. I tack up the pictures of Donald Duck that I drag around with me in an effort to recreate a familiar universe.

The skylight is too high to see anything through it except a patch of black sky. I concentrate on this rectangle. What if my mother rented room 22? Where would we go then?

6

I love my little sister. I'm glad she's here, life isn't as cold. My mother finds it amusing to tell how when I was two years old she found me trying to strangle baby Marianne. That story doesn't make me laugh. I was jealous, it seems. Strangle Marianne? No, I would miss her. I prefer to pull her ear or pinch her chubby cheeks, not really hurting her, just reminding her firmly that I'm the eldest, the strongest, that we are here for each other.

We don't hug in my family. Physical contact is reduced to a minimum. Touching would be letting the body express its tenderness, and what's the point of that? Work, bustle and distance act as a substitute for everything.

'Do you have to touch each other to make babies?' I ask, curious.

My mother is embarrassed and tells me her cabbage-patch theory. Aunt Mary cracks up. How strange, I think to myself.

Tonight the hotel has lapsed into its night-time silence. I can't sleep and I am listening out for the slightest sound, the potential movement of the china doorknob. I'm watching for my mother's exhausted face, for it to come round the door and ask us to leave our room, whatever the time and the depth of my sister's sleep, to go even higher, even further, into a space so small we can hardly fit, so small there could be no smaller space. We would be invisible, forgotten forever.

This childhood moving of rooms orchestrated by my mother, these nocturnal migrations to make way for strangers for the sake of a few extra florins, leave me with a deep conviction that sometimes eats into me beneath my calm façade: I'm in the way, too much, cheap, cut-price. I wander from room to room.

7

'Is Hans here?' asks the customer.

'No, he no longer works here.' Aunt Alice's voice is terse.

The customer is surprised, his hands trembling on the reception counter.

'But where has he gone?' he persists, mournfully.

'We don't know, and do not wish to know.'

'Very well . . .'

The customer takes his key and starts up the stairs. He hesitates, stops, grabs the banister, and brings a hand to his face. We are watching him.

'Surely he's not crying?' asks Aunt Alice. 'Do you know him?'

'No.'

I go off to pace up and down the lounge. Yes, I know him. I recognise that scarlet coat with the black fur collar, that skin blistered with rampant acne. It's the man that 'Uncle' Hans used to kiss in the kitchen. I had walked in silently, thinking I was alone, it was late and I hadn't eaten. 'Uncle' Hans was holding the man by the neck, clasping him, eating the man's mouth. Their movements were intense, they seemed to be hungry for each other. The man had his back to me. 'Uncle' Hans was facing me. He saw me immediately, paused for a moment, then resumed his gobbling of the man's mouth. They were moaning a little. 'Uncle' Hans held my fixed gaze, then shut his eyes, and reopened them straight onto me. He stared as if he wanted to scream something at me, his suppressed rage perhaps, his desire to see my bubble explode, my sheltered, mute, dreamy little girl's world.

I was witnessing desire and I didn't like it. I was hearing pleasure and it wasn't nice. I inched imperceptibly backwards, holding 'Uncle' Hans's gaze.

My soles skated along the lino as I noiselessly left that invisible circle created around two bodies that wanted each other. I had walked into intimacy and I walked straight back out again.

I often ask myself about this world that comes to life so noisily behind closed doors. What are they doing? Personally, I always prefer a bit of light, a door ajar, so I can glimpse other people's lives, like old people at windows. Doors close on intimacy, desire, secrets.

I pay attention to everything. I have noticed that there's an energy stronger than anything else, which brings people together at nightfall, when work and the noise of the city cease. It magnetises them. In the bar I watch bodies touch each other under tables, see women offer up their necks. It's an adult energy about which I am curious.

Why are my mother and father exempt from this energy? Why don't they come together? My mother doesn't offer her neck up like the other women. No, my parents don't embrace, not even behind their bedroom door. I know. My brother sleeps in their room. I walk in there without knocking, quietly, apparently innocent and lost, determined to find out the truth.

My parents are rarely in there together. Callas the dog growls and guards my father closely.

My parents are always heading in opposite directions. When my mother goes to bed, my father gets up. When my father undresses, my mother is waking up. There is no circle around them, no intimacy.

8

Aunt Alice is as upright and well behaved as Aunt Mary is unpredictable, unique and crazy.

Aunt Alice is my mother's sister. She arrives early each morning by train from Hilversum (about fifteen miles away) to work at the hotel. She lives with her mother, my pious, Protestant, austere, taciturn, good grandmother.

Sometimes, I leave the bustle of the hotel to seek refuge with her. I took the train by myself for the first time aged four. With the wind in the right direction I could hear the train departure announcements quite clearly. I thought they were calling me so I left without a word, a little doll, small, resolute and self-propelled.

'Stand back from the platform edge, the Hilversum train is about to depart!'

This time I am on board, a little girl who intrigues the other passengers.

My grandmother has principles. In contrast to the murky busyness of the hotel, she gives clarity and rules to my childhood: something to lean on.

No noise on Sundays at Granny's house, no bicycle. The table is a place of quiet, not a station chip shop. You must meditate and pray so as not to burn in the flames of hell. You thank God at every meal as if He were providing the food

Himself. It's strange. I sense that my questions would not be welcome in this slightly strained silence, so I keep quiet, I obey, that's why I'm here.

There's a three-sided mirror in front of my chair. I always make sure I can see it, training my curiosity on myself. I peer at my reflection, discovering myself a little more each time. An often solitary child, I am interested in myself. I look at my profile, the top of my head, the usually invisible parts of myself. I also watch myself grow. And the bigger I grow, the more I watch myself. I like looking at myself. When my grandmother isn't there I go right up to the mirror, so close I could kiss it. My breath creates a light mist that I wipe away with an arm so I can find myself again. I move each of my features in turn, making all kinds of false faces that I hold for a few moments. Pretending is easy.

I'm intrigued by the colour of my eyes, by the family resemblance. I don't know the name of this colour. Grey, pale green . . . ?

My grandmother doesn't like my narcissistic ways, my poses. This lengthy contemplation of my face, its discovery from every angle, distracts me from my prayer and is really too much. So one day Granny stands up, tacks some newspaper over the mirror and looks at me with kindly authority, not saying a word. Deprived of the sight of myself, for a few days of the holidays I surrender to my grandmother's good, serene orderliness.

9

Aunt Mary is manic-depressive, like her father.

'She's not very well in the head,' my mother whispers.

Before she came to the hotel we used to visit this bizarre aunt in hospital. She seemed normal, all smiley and sweet. Aunt Mary enjoyed our visits and always made sure to put on a good show, to prove her sanity and that she shouldn't be locked up. Depending on her state she was either drowned in lithium or subject to electroshock therapy to achieve an artificial stability. I was little, and struck by the size of the nurses.

'They're animals!' she would say, quietly so they wouldn't hear. In a bid for survival she set her bed on fire and was asked to leave. My father went to get her. He signed a document, paid for the burnt bed and brought Aunt Mary back to the hotel.

She was shouting 'Tell me I'm not crazy, tell me!' as she left the hospital, furious at having been pharmaceutically gagged, reduced to a state of continual and hazy smiling. She jabbed a vengeful finger at the huge, impassive white figures.

'No, you're not crazy,' my father replied, squeezing her hand. 'Come on, let's go!'

'Manic-depressive' is an odd, complex word, with an intellectual sound to it. It is always said clearly but quietly, accompanied by sorrowful discomfort on my mother's face. It must be a failing that needs to be hidden, a rare defect that has affected our family, of which my aunt is the vivid proof.

Aunt Mary spends half her life in the air and the rest on the floor. She lives mostly at night, when the contrasts show less. She sometimes laughs and sings for days at a time, buying extravagant presents on credit and exclaiming at how wonderful life is, and how short. Aunt Mary gives her love in huge bouquets, or else goes to ground, at her slowest moments, like the victim of a broken dream or departed lover. Then one day she comes back to life, believing in it again, more fervently than ever. Giving us her sense of humour, her regained appetite and her temporary zest for life.

When I grow up I'm going to be manic-depressive. It's so much fun, so entertaining.

I adore my aunts. So opposite to each other, but always there for little love-starved me. They are the warm, lively figures of my daily life, weaving a palpable web of love around me every day.

Aunt Mary runs the hotel bar, that pivotal space she often doesn't close until morning, that hub of routine, ritual debauchery. She doesn't sleep much, or drink at all. Aunt Mary is always sober as she witnesses the spectacle of the daily drinking sessions. The customers feel relaxed around this kindly, changeable woman – to the extent that some of them think her as drunk as them.

My mother is a regular, discreet, efficient customer at the bar. She drinks constantly, serving herself wine or sherry. She can hold her alcohol – I take after her. She never seems drunk. When she is, she hides away or tells me to go to my room.

That's all my mother seems able to say whenever she is vulnerable, moved or surprised.

My mother is incapable of expressing emotion. She suppresses it as a weakness, a threat. Life is hard and dangerous, you have to be on guard. My mother fears feelings, as a never-ending wave sure to sweep her away. She prefers control, and uses drink to make this inhuman state bearable.

My father frequents the bar for the same reasons as my mother, but he also hosts the space. He plays the piano and the synthesiser, a sort of modern music box that reproduces the sounds of other instruments as well as bespoke rhythms. It is magical, mysterious, cheerful. My father occasionally and impatiently teaches me a little.

The customers like the hotel bar, where everyone drinks until they are laughing uncontrollably at nothing; deep, throaty laughs that resonate through the whole building. Some fall over, and weep, then get up again and sing, badly. They shout unknown names – faraway lands they will visit, women they will love.

10

Alcohol has been part of my life since the day when, before I was weaned, my mother got me to sleep by putting a cognac-soaked cloth wrapped around a lump of sugar to my lips.

Alcohol made my father loud and cheerful. He played, sang, acted the fool; he was my clown.

Alcohol broke through my mother's Protestant restraint, brought her out of her silence, freed up unknown, vicious words, the words of a different person. Emotions burst forth, and then my mother would disappear.

Alcohol gave life. It was the song, the blood, the bond of the hotel. My father would drink up to forty beers a day. I practised my maths by counting them. To arrive at different totals I would then add each whole glass of cognac and each Underberg to the beers.

When he was sober, my father didn't speak.

I preferred alcohol to silence.

11

Kristel is my real name, from the word 'crystal'. It suited my father's fragile luminosity.

There's not always a reason for fragility, it can just be a part of someone's nature. My father was fragile but he hid it, drowning and destroying himself in alcohol and noise. My father adored clay-pigeon shooting and hunting, and his carpentry machines – the screaming metal beasts that lived in his refuge, the attic. He would listen to the intolerable mechanical roar of these carving tools without ear protection.

When out hunting he would fire his gun often, right next to his ears, shooting rebelliously in the air out of a taste for loud noises. By middle age he was almost deaf, which suited him. The voices of the women, the cries and screaming of the children, these signs of life slowly disappeared, growing fainter like an echo, vanishing into his silence and leaving him in his chosen solitude.

My father had not been a child. He was sent to boarding school at four years old. I imagine him as a brave little chap, clever, forced to act grown up, to make his bed without creases, not to cry at an age when that's all you can do. He grew up alone, with no protection, never carefree. He discovered desire before love, and alcohol first of all.

My father drank, hunted, loved the sea, sport, flesh and

chess. In Dutch chess is called *schaken*, which also refers to the abduction of a sweet young girl by a nasty man.

Perhaps my father thought he was nasty, but he wasn't. Just broken and mostly absent.

In his attic he makes chess figurines. There are hundreds of them, arranged according to size and by category: queens, castles, pawns, bishops. The best ones in front, the flawed hidden behind. There's no end to this manic creativity, or to my father's obsession with this game, this strategic battle, this checkmate.

Sometimes when I'm bored I go up there to see him, daring to enter. He stops his machine and sits motionless, looking at me. I smile at him, feeling like his prettiest figurine. He points out his new creations then quickly starts work again, and I clear off to escape the racket.

My father was Catholic, the son of a hotel-owner and a musician. My grandfather ran an orchestra, and once brought back with him from a trip to Switzerland a strange, unique instrument that made the sound of a fairy tale: a xylophone. It drew people from all around.

My mother came from a humble peasant background, she was a Calvinist and very beautiful. She was brought up strictly by her widowed mother, to an extremely harsh religious code. Fear of divine punishment replaced a father's discipline.

I remember my mother when she was young; she was fluid as a bohemian dancer, charming and stylish as a movie star. My parents met at a ball. They danced together for a long time, floating, dazzled. My father loved women, and beauty; he loved my mother from that first dance.

Mum loved dancing, it was her element. Her other loves were dressmaking, work and my father. She wasn't very religious. Marriage gave her an escape from religious excess and the fear of God. She preferred profane to divine love, and converted to Catholicism out of faith in my father. My mother didn't go to Mass, but made us keep that weekly ritual in her place.

I loved this Sunday outing. At the end of the ceremony I would smile angelically and sidle up to the collection plates to pinch the money I sometimes found there. I would shake the collection boxes and force open their ridiculous little lids, then take my sister to the movies to watch Laurel and Hardy. Much more fun.

12

Once she was a wife and mother – just a few years after that first ball – my mother stopped dancing. She worked. My mother no longer did the thing she loved. She became obsessed by the beneficial effects of hard toil, austere as a matter of duty, irritable, often sad as she witnessed my father's slow flight.

She concentrated on her daily tasks, on the hotel and her children. She concerned herself with our homework, our health, our cleanliness and the perfect ironing of our clothes, which she often made – with some skill – herself. My mother was unable to express her affection other than through faultless material care. We were scattered around so as not to disturb hotel business. I was often in my bedroom, Marianne with our neighbours – kind, cigar-selling shopkeepers – and my brother wherever he pleased. He was the family's little man; he called the shots.

People say they miss the deceased. I missed my father and my mother when they were still fully alive. They travelled through my childhood in the same way they moved around the hotel: my mother industrious, hurried, hidden; my father drunk, flamboyant, alone.

13

'Mrs Kristel?! Mrs Kristel?!'

The man in the hotel lobby is getting upset. It's Mr Janssen, who runs the newspaper shop across the street from the hotel. Aunt Mary hurries off to find my mother, who comes down looking surprised, a chrome thimble on her finger.

'Yes, Mr Janssen, what can I do for you?' she asks nervously.

'Keep your girls under control, Mrs Kristel! Keep them under control!'

'Whatever do you mean?'

'How old are they, now?'

'Sylvia will be ten this autumn and Marianne is eight, why?'

'Ten and eight . . . well, it doesn't augur . . .'

'What doesn't it augur?' My mother is getting impatient.

'It just doesn't augur well, that's all!'

My mother turns towards me and starts interrogating me.

'What have you done?'

'Nothing.'

'Nothing?!'

Mr Janssen interrupts me.

'Mrs Kristel, since the beginning of the summer your daughter and her little sister have been cavorting on the tables of your restaurant. At around 3 p.m., when the room is empty. Laughing, singing, gesticulating –'

'But they are children, Mr Janssen!' my mother cuts in. 'Children do play and dance!'

'Yes, but not naked! Totally naked! They undress and parade around, stroking themselves and wiggling about so outrageously that passers-by stare, and then bash into the telephone box! Look, the glass panel has broken! Your daughters find it amusing, especially the older one. If the collision is violent, they leap off the table like fleas and scarper. I'm the only one who's seen what they're up to. Don't you hear them?! They sing their heads off, which is to say they screech. I can hear them through an open window on the other side of the road! I haven't said anything until now, but I'm warning you –'

My mother interrupts Mr Janssen again.

'OK, Mr Janssen, OK. Please forgive us, I'm very sorry. Sylvia sometimes likes to draw attention to herself, you know how they can be at her age, and her sister is still young and easily influenced . . . but it won't happen again.'

The neighbour goes off, shaking his head and still muttering: 'Ten and eight . . .'

My mother is bright red. Her time has been wasted and her local reputation trashed. She runs around the hotel screaming and foaming at the mouth. She is tracking me down, full of threats.

'Sylvia! Sylvia! If you don't come here right now . . .'

But I've been out of there for a while. It had been obvious that Mr Janssen wasn't coming over to discuss the day's gossip. I am crouched down in my new hiding place, the cupboard on the half-landing of the stairs. Aunt Alice knows but she doesn't let on. She has seen me and has stationed herself just in front, with her back to the cupboard.

'Where is Sylvia?! Do you know where she is, or what?!'

My mother's rage isn't passing. She has armed herself with the big willow carpet-beater she uses on the mattresses, and of course her long pointy nails that pierce the skin like staples. She threatens Aunt Alice, throwing her hands up in the air and yelling that she 'didn't deserve this'!

I stay in that cupboard for two hours, not making a sound. My mother is bound to calm down eventually. It is a matter of time. Soon she will get out the little steel goblet she hides in her sewing box like an oversized thimble, and drink dozens of small sips of sherry or white wine, sometimes even the whole bottle – but by thimbleful, persuading herself that these sips added up to less than the whole. She will fall asleep, shattered, beaten and drunk. She will forget. I will escape the willow whip.

So Mr Nosy's nose exploded like a ripe fruit? Tough luck. I am up for anything to avoid boredom and get some attention.

My brother has found another, effective way of getting attention. He shapes his faeces into little geometric sculptures that he attempts to stick to the walls, laughing and running off with dirty hands and stripes on his face like an Indian. My mother swears and rages, apologises to the customers, pleads her helplessness with a sponge in her hand. Marianne spends more and more time at the neighbours' house with her friend Anneke. They are as thick as thieves. When I bump into her in the hotel she smiles at me. She gives off a mysterious smell of tobacco these days. She seems happy with her life next door.

14

'I hate penetration! Do you understand?'

My mother is drunk. She has taken me by the shoulders and is staring at me fixedly, repeating: 'I hate penetration. I can't stand your father coming back from hunting or wherever, reeking of alcohol, sweat and blood, slipping into my bed while I sleep and wanting to penetrate me. I'm sleeping, tired, and he is all dirty and excited and wants to penetrate me. I don't want it, I can't do it. I'm too tight, do you understand?!'

'No, I don't understand, Mummy.'

'You do, you do understand! And anyway, there isn't just penetration, there are other things you can do . . .'

I wriggle out of her arms, put my hands over my ears and shout, as I run away: 'I don't understand! I don't understand what you're talking about, so stop talking to me like this, leave me alone, Mummy!'

When she is drunk, lost and abandoned, when my father has gone off, when she has refused herself to him, my mother talks to me without any concept of the child I still am. She is confiding in a human being, perhaps the closest one to her, confessing her pain. I run away. I cannot hear these adult words, nor contemplate that my father and mother can no longer stand each other.

My mother insists that she has never made love with my

father. She denies any physical relationship, any contact. She doesn't know how we were born; not from her body in any case.

I am the eldest. I have two years on Marianne and four on my brother, but I still can't remember my mother pregnant. Perhaps she hid her round belly under artfully loose home-made dresses? She must have bound her belly, smoothing it out like a mouldable paste, moulding us too, rejecting this evidence of the other's body, this visible proof of her pene-tration, her lack of restraint. I have no memory of childbirth, or preparations, or a wait, or her absence; just squalling, ugly newborns who scared me and were presented by Aunt Alice as holy marvels.

15

I am jealous of my sister. She has found in the neighbours a
warm and loving foster-family. I am occasionally invited to
dinner. I hang around, trying to get myself adopted too, but
I am already big and independent. I have my own friend, but
she is cruel. Her parents own one of the very first televisions in
Utrecht. I am fascinated, bewitched. She knows it, and invites
me over when she wants to and pointedly not when I am dying
to go. I am devastated. My mother feels sorry for me and
understands that she can make up for her absence by providing
me with this piece of modern treasure. My mother buys a
television! A box of marvels, a miracle; never-ending pictures.
It lives in my parents' bedroom. I watch it as much as I can.
My mother puts limits on my hypnosis, especially in the
evenings. I must go to bed. Once in my room I keep quiet for a
few moments, giving the impression that I've fallen asleep,
then tiptoe back out again in the direction of the television.
The door of my parents' bedroom is closed but glazed, with a
multicoloured stained-glass window in the middle. I stand
stock-still a few feet behind the door, just able to see the TV,
distorted but in colour.

I am growing up alone these days. Marianne is almost never
around, Nicolas spends his life outside and my parents are
becoming invisible. I don't deal with it well. I rebel. At school,

I refuse to go to the toilet during the allotted break times. My bladder becomes infected but I still refuse to go. I won't hang my clothes on the coat rack. I hate the squirrel design on it, that pseudo-sweet animal with claws like my mother's staples.

I become a stubborn, contrary child.

I never do what I'm told, rejecting everything wholesale. Hierarchies and orders remind me of my mother. Growing up is a dead end. I won't take the boring educational path I'm being shown, won't heed the stupid, abstract advice, 'you should do this, a big girl must do that ...' But what is a big girl? A woman who works herself to the bone? A woman who has forgotten how to laugh or dance, who says she isn't a woman? Nothing about grown bodies or adults holds my interest. I like only my childhood books, my continuing dreams at the window, my Walt Disney pictures, the movies and TV. I become lazy, indolent; I still am, sometimes.

I have a need to lie down and do nothing, motionless, watching the time passing, experiencing idleness, gazing around the room with slow-motion eyes, my only activity the gentle coming and going of air in my chest. I like being inert, touching the slow moment. I am congealing in torpor, in rest, becoming stunted. I convince myself of my innocent stillness, my different fate: I am not behaving like my mother, am not trapped in the industrious rhythm of life, on and on until death.

It's around then that I start dreaming of a job in which I do nothing. A task that won't exhaust, won't cause black rings under my eyes, on the contrary will make them shine. A soft, joyful job, rather languid and voluptuous.

Marianne no longer comes to the hotel even at night. I sleep alone. I bumped into her today on my way to the chip shop.

She looked my way so I slipped my arm through hers. She looked at me nastily and said: 'Let me go! I'm not your sister! I am Marianne Van de Berg, Anneke is my sister, not you!' I let go of her arm, fled to the hotel and wept. I've got a new book: *Billy Bradley Goes to Boarding School.* Good idea. I've nothing left to lose, it can only be better than here. I ask to go away to school, an immediate escape.

16

'May I have a cognac, please?' I speak up to hide my nervousness.

'A cognac?! You must be joking, my girl! And you'll sing a little lower, if you don't mind!'

This funny Flemish expression means 'lower your voice'. I wasn't singing, I didn't feel like it. I am afraid of this new life, afraid that I have lost my head and made a bad decision.

I am eleven years old, it's my first night at boarding school and I can't sleep. This is the first time I've been refused a cognac. They've also refused to take my bags up. What is this place?

'Straight to the sickroom with you, my girl!'

Sister Assissia is shocked, and wants to be sure I am of sound mind.

I am sane and realise for the first time, from the astounded look of this strict but kindly adult, that the relationship between alcohol and the body is an unnatural one, that the two are not bound together like the body and water. Alcohol is not merely a bracing liquid that stings and warms, leaving you dizzy and making you sing even if you're tone-deaf.

Alcohol is not natural, not good.

I am returned to my room.

'So, no cognac, my girl. But three Hail Marys and two Paters will send you to sleep just as well!'

Sister Assissia shows me my room, shuts the door behind her and rushes off, bemused, thinking of the vast amount of work that will be needed to sort me out.

This is a religious secondary boarding school, not far from Utrecht. I am now in a finishing school for smart young ladies preparing for life as upper-class wives.

At the hotel, when I couldn't sleep I used to either serve myself a small cognac or finish off the customers' glasses, making crazy mixtures that knocked me out fast. I was sometimes upset in the evenings, left alone to face the issues confronting a growing girl. I would feel sad when I heard them announce the departure of the last train for Hilversum.

The girls in the other rooms must be asleep but I am not. I open the window. There's no station here, no noise, the silence is total. The air is so bracing and clean it makes my head spin. I cannot believe Utrecht is only a few miles away. I'm in the middle of nowhere, here. A few bats beat the night sky slowly with their pointy wings. No red Coca-Cola signs; just a faint gleam, down and to the left at the entrance to the school, lighting up the notice 'Do not walk on the grass'. You have to take the gravel track, the straight and narrow path that leads to the road and the trees, the tall, dark, still trees waiting to take back their earth.

No walking on the lawn, no cognac, no being up at this late hour. I come from a world in which anything is allowed, except dancing naked and slobbering on my cheek. The change is harsh. Sister Assissia is doing her rounds. I can hear her tired step and the clink of the crucifix that hangs down her front. I quickly turn off the light and slip under the covers fully dressed. I lie still, listening to the doorknob creak like at the hotel. The door closes and the steps move away. I will not have to change rooms. I am alone and without alcohol. The merry-go-round in my head spins ever faster. The Square's neon sign is a bright flame that dazzles me when I close my eyes. My father's laughter and the cries of the station make me dizzy. I am discovering silence, and absence. I didn't see much of my parents but I knew they were there, at the end of the corridor or in the attic, and my aunts were close by too. At the hotel there were bits of love scattered around like jigsaw pieces, for me to put together again each day. It was my bright red fairground, the unique place in which I had landed. I had got used to it, as only children can.

I will get used to these prison-bar trees, this forbidden lawn, the holy water. I am eleven years old, I will get used to anything, just about.

I find the 6 a.m. wake-up call hard. Fasting through Mass every day so as to be pure before God makes me weak. The costumed people, the high-pitched, loud singing and the mysterious dance in a mist of incense all combine to make me dizzy. After a few days of this the tired, upset and lazy girl faints. Back to the sickroom, pale and limp but away from Mass and the wake-up call. At night, with a torch under the covers, I read a book about cowboys and Indians – free, lively and wild.

17

'Kristel! Stand up straight! Always stand up straight, girls! The world is not on your shoulders but under your feet!'

Sister Marie Immaculata strives to teach us good manners.

Marie Immaculata ... what a pretty name. Pure and dignified, like her. Is it an adopted name, a stage name? What is the real name of this pale, virgin Marie Immaculata? Who is she?

'Stand tall! Hold your head high! It's not what's on the ground that's nigh!'

Sister Marie Immaculata is uncompromising, and good.

I have always stood up straight. I find it impossible to slouch – Sister Marie's classes have helped me to hold myself well throughout my life, whatever the situation. Stay upright, look strong, give the impression of being so at all times. My dancer's bearing has given my chaotic life some style, some tautness, a slightly aloof elegance that has borne me aloft, held high, out of reach of the vulgar and commonplace.

I stood straight, but I was clumsy. I struggled to hold a fork well, and the whole class used to laugh at me. Food spurted easily off my plate, I was always staining my neighbours' clothes. I was happy to learn grace but not to bend myself to these daunting and ridiculous rules about table manners: start with the outermost knife and fork, then, with each dish, move in towards the plate, then, delicately, take the water glass by its stem, not the wine glass first like a drunkard, then, delicately, bring it to your lips.

'And not the other way round, girls!'

I was distracted. I would go straight to the fish fork, which had the least sharp teeth. I didn't like the other one; it was 'Uncle' Hans's fork. I would bump the stem of my glass, creating a rhythm as shrill as my grandfather's xylophone, driving the priestess of good manners crazy.

On Saturdays the daughters of ministers and diplomats drove off in a lovely, dreamlike procession of limousines. I stayed put, or took the train for my Utrecht station.

18

'Kristel! Post!'

Sister Marie Immaculata has a pseudo-strict manner that belies her sweetness and helps her keep order. She knows how important post is – it's obvious from the silent gathering of usually boisterous girls. The unruly herd has miraculously transformed into waiting rows of ramrod-straight little grey stakes. We all want to know if we still exist in the outside world. My mother has written to me, as she does every week, the content always similar – what's happening at the hotel, Dad, Aunt Mary's moods, and the weather in Utrecht, as if it were different to here. I should have had a postbox at the hotel. Would my mother have put a daily letter in it? Perhaps she needs this modest distance, this absence, in order to write the words she doesn't say.

My mother's letters are colourful. Aunt Mary knocked out a drunken customer who wanted to take her upstairs. The hotel boiler broke suddenly, making the temperature plummet and the customers flee. My father is away more and more, likewise searching for a little warmth.

I like these letters. The softness of the paper, my mother folded between my fingers. Often there are crossings-out and the faint smell of sherry, and stains blurring her neat handwriting. I wait eagerly for these letters, this belated attention.

My mother never saw how happy her dull words made me, how I wrung my hands as I waited and smiled when my name was called. Every week I hung on the pretty lips and perfect diction of Sister Marie Immaculata.

I have a good time at this strange boarding school, imposing my passive rule, spending cheerful, normal, sporty years there. Running, swimming, jumping. Letting off steam, making my changing body move and sweat.

I start smoking. Even the sisters smoke on Sundays. Like my father I favour filterless Camels, whose strong smoke scratches my throat. I am proud of this adult act that I can accomplish without coughing, tough like him.

Is there any option but to behave like your father, and mother? Can one break with this need to belong? Perhaps with age and the ravages of poor imitation.

The maths teacher is called Hees Been. He has a gammy leg which makes him wince when he stretches it out. He is fairly young, and more interested in the changing curves of our bodies than in geometry. He has a long lock of plastered-back hair, on which he unconsciously wipes his snot when he sneezes. I enjoy playing with this easy prey, making him pay for my disgust. I fold over my waistband to make my skirt as short as possible, then retrieve imaginary bits of chalk from the floor, bending gently in two, sensing the top of my thighs becoming visible, feeling the cool air on the lower parts of my bottom and watching the teacher's face turn red. He says nothing, he is watching me, my buttocks are a vision to behold. His confusion and my power make me feel good. Everyone is laughing and I smother my own giggles with my back to the class. Then, stunned and naive, I sit back down in the first row, inhabited by the short-sighted and those whose surnames begin with A. I am delighted with my demonstration – if not mathematical then at least physiological.

Sister Gertrude speaks to us in perfect Queen's English. I like the language, and soon realise that it's the key to getting away. Sister Gertrude's hairstyle is a black-and-white rectangle perfectly aligned with the dark arm of her steel spectacles, making her resemble a shoebox. Sister Gertrude is ugly, but kind.

My father says you have to be ugly to become a nun.

Sister Marie Andrée teaches French and history. She tells us about the war in her warm, solemn, captivating voice. With her class unusually silent she describes the never-forgiven invasion, the suffering of a nation, the confiscated bicycles, the people starving to death and eating grated tulip bulbs.

That cruel, intimate image stayed with me for a long time. Lovely bright tulips, twofold and useful. At flower shops I sometimes imagine being given the option: 'Would you like your tulips grated, Ms Kristel, or in a bouquet?'

My mother talked to us about the war, too. At a very young age she used to go off on her wooden-wheeled bicycle – there weren't any tyres left – and cycle for hours to swap a piece of silverware for some potatoes. One night, exhausted and empty-bellied, she had knocked on a farmhouse door and pleaded her hunger. The generous peasant woman sat her down at the table and gave her a melted-cheese pancake so rich, so big for that concave belly that my mother was ill for several days, and had to stay at the woman's house. My mother used to say that she was going to find her, so she could thank her and take the opportunity to have her to stay instead.

Dutch people are thrifty and they bear grudges; on holiday in Germany they're still prone to exclaim, 'Give me back my bicycle!' Mine had stayed at the hotel. Just as well – I was always falling off because I was so dreamy and lazy I had forgotten to pedal.

Father Gianotten is so modern and believes so much in love – 'because God is love' – that he has married one of the schoolgirls.

Sister Christine bears the heavy burden of our sexual education. She is clearly overwhelmed by this unrequested mission, and speaks in a brittle monotone of a threatening world. Men are governed by uncontrollable urges due to the hormones that run through their veins like poison, and women spend their lives trying to escape these male urges. The rest – the detail, the reproductive technique necessary for humanity's survival – is in Latin. Those whistling words are messengers from another world; they leave me pensive.

19

'Kristel! Post!'

The tone of my mother's letter is new, the stains many, the words hard to decipher. Have they been blurred by alcohol, or tears? I cannot understand them all. My mother is devastated, screaming her despair: my father has a mistress, not a passing fling but a woman who is winning his heart, who wants him. The words are rough, coarse, my mother is wrecked. I am terror-stricken. Sister Marie Immaculata grabs my letter, reads it and turns pale.

'These words are not appropriate for you, Sylvia. I will call your mother and speak to her. Calm yourself.'

I forget the letter. It will soon be the holidays. I perfect my manners and carry on having a good time.

'The man must enter the restaurant first!'

'But isn't he supposed to hold the door for the ladies, Sister?'

'No! The man protects the woman. When entering an unknown space he is firstly making sure that people's attention will fall on him rather than the naturally shy and reserved woman. Yes, I am saying shy and reserved! Secondly, he is checking that there are no crooks inside. Evil is everywhere, and the man protects the woman from evil . . .'

I have always waited at restaurant doors to check whether

the man had manners. Whether he would protect me or let me walk in as if brandishing a trophy.

I now have a little group of followers at boarding school. They gaze at me, and listen rapt to my risqué stories. I tell them about the hotel, its pulsating, unusual life, everything I've seen there, everything I've learned about men and women. The striptease customer with her boa, who compèred the staff party and tried in vain to seduce 'Uncle' Hans. The secret world of transitory customers, freedom re-found for a single night in an isolated space – a hotel room is a parallel, distant world. I mime the faces of the chambermaids as they discover stains while stripping the beds. I reveal the complex stories of my world, so different to the one in which we live. I speak of life as it really is, not in theory, not in Latin.

The nuns reprimand me:

'There's nothing to be proud of about coming from such a circus, my girl!'

They want to protect me, in their simple, boundaried way, from a confused adult world in which I might go astray.

One must pray for life to be nothing but love.

20

It is summer and I'm back at the hotel.

We're going to the seaside for a few days; my father has rented us a sweet little house. Aunt Mary is coming too. In the car my mother says nothing. She opens the window, taking great gulps of the warm air and staring fixedly at the clear sky. My father regularly informs us of the number of miles still to go. His voice is unusually monotonous. Marianne is sad to have left Anneke, and my brother is leaning on the back shelf guessing the makes of the passing cars. Aunt Mary is dozing. I watch the treeless fields rush by, perfectly fenced flat rectangles in single but various colours. Night is slowly falling. What silence, for the holidays!

We have barely arrived when my father tells us that tomorrow morning he will be making an important announcement, for which he will wake us up. But now it's bedtime. Aunt Mary is prostrate; she's in a low phase. My mother goes straight to her room without checking the house as she usually does, without sweeping or inspecting the fridge. The furniture is covered in sheets. I entertain myself by waving them through the air in a great cloud of dust that makes Aunt Mary cough. At last some movement, some noise!

In the bedroom Marianne is not asleep. She asks me about boarding school. Do I have any new friends? She has grown up, and tells me that she's already tried smoking. I scold her, smiling, happy that she's sharing my room as before. I grab her ear in gentle revenge for her desertion. She pretends that it hurts. We have a singing competition; she starts with a musical film she's already seen three times, *The Sound of Music*. I laugh – I've seen the film and it's delightful, but it's a kids' film! My sister doesn't understand the English words but the rousing, simple tunes – joyful lullabies – have seeped into her like a divine message. Marianne stands on the bed and apes Julie Andrews in that scene where the kindly governess attempts to distract seven half-orphaned children terrified by the storm: '*Cream-coloured ponies and crisp apple strudels ... these are a few of my favourite things ... when the dog bites, when the bee stings ...*' Julie teaches the children that when life becomes hard you have to think of simple, good things to drive away the fear. I tease my sister but I must admit that many years later I can still remember every word of that wonderful song, which I've sung far more often than I've ever prayed.

'*Krim kolor poni! ...*' Marianne sings her beloved gobble-degook over and over again. I interrupt to launch into my grown-up Beatles songs, demonstrating my mastery of English to this uncultured little kid. Then I tell her it's time to sleep – and Marianne obeys me. I go to the window, the sea is rough and the gulls are circling and crying.

'Stormy weather, stormy weather ...' mutters Aunt Mary in the corridor, sounding like a ghost.

I can't sleep. My father wants to make an important announcement. Is he going to sell the hotel? Is he ill? Does he not want us any more? I am worried, tossing restlessly as if I were at sea.

I have left the door open and can hear my mother's voice, much quieter than usual. I move towards the corridor and listen to her whispering on and on. I can't make out the words but I get a sense of the tone. She seems to be questioning my father, who isn't replying; she is pleading with him.

It is morning. I haven't slept much. My father comes in and wakes us rather curtly. My mother is in the kitchen, she hasn't put on her flowery, sleeveless summer dress. She seems to be cold, and kisses us without looking at us.

There's a ring at the door. I jump, the chime is loud and unexpected. Aunt Mary suddenly wakes up on her chair, grumbles and goes to answer. I hear shouting. We rush to the door to see a white-faced woman. Hanny's eyes are outlined in black, her lips are thin and bright red and her backcombed hair has been pulled up into a huge round beehive on the top of her head, and sprayed solid. I take a step backwards, she looks like a witch. My father moves Aunt Mary out of the way and invites the woman in. My mother comes out of the kitchen, stands behind my father and looks away.

'Children, this is my new wife!'

My mother doesn't say anything. She has known for a few days, and she has relented; she accepts everything, it seems.

Aunt Mary screams and flies into a rage, grabbing the sherry bottle by the living-room door and whacking the woman on the head with it, like in a cartoon. The woman emits funny little shrieks and extricates herself, unhurt. Her beehive has acted as a buffer. My father grasps his sister round the waist and takes her to her room, then sits down wearily. The woman is looking at me with a faint smile.

It's not possible. It can't be! In this moment, right here,

right now, if I rush at my father, telling him how much I love him and begging him to keep my mother, he will do it. He has to, he will listen to his daughter. I jump on his knee and plead.

'Daddy, no! You can't do this!'

I shake his heavy shoulders. He bursts into sobs, avoiding my kisses and saying in a broken voice: 'But I'm weak, my little one, weak . . .'

My father has chosen. The woman continues to smile. Her hair is slightly dishevelled but she is standing firm, solid. Blood rushes to my brain. I see red. I am full of rage, concentrated and built up over fourteen years. I am a bloodthirsty lion. I pounce on the witch, punching and scratching her, pulling at her plastic bun, calling her a whore – that new, never-spoken word. I want to kill her, slaughter her, exterminate her.

My mother and father eventually manage to control me. The woman is knocked to the ground but is not crying. Tough, despicable creature, uncrushable insect. I am shut in my room for the rest of the day. I bash on the door, yelling and crying, then suddenly stop. I take myself back in hand. Hold my head high. 'Stand tall, hold your head up . . .'

I tell myself that there's no point, that I must accept this split as an inexplicable but possible and natural part of life. Tomorrow the rough sea might be smooth as velvet. My father is leaving. It must be the time of year. You think you can control love, life, bonds, you think you are building something, but in fact it's all just seasons passing.

What will happen now? I don't know. I'm afraid of the next phase in this dissolved life. You have to accept that there's no sense to life, that nature is absurd and changeable. You have to carry on, struggling along between sun and bad weather, between the first ball and the last dance.

21

My parents got divorced. That's it, that's what's happened. Disunited, for life. It was my brave mother who officially told me. I am the oldest, entitled to responsibility, to scolding and to announcements, from the most trivial to the most serious. My parents have divorced. I am a neutral, one-way receptacle of news, of sharp wounds and of this announcement which has broken the thread of a life, devastated its shape and coherence.

We had been a scattered family, rather drunken, our bond one of industrious indifference and chaste, silent proximity. Work, introversion, the impossibility of really meeting and an incapacity for warm-heartedness had kept us at a distance from each other. We had been a family as bruised and divided as war veterans, but a family nonetheless.

My mother says that it doesn't matter, that God will take care of us. God won't do a thing, and neither will my mother. I see how hurt she is: she trembles all the time and her eyes shirk contact, blinking away her tears so they don't fall. My mother wants to be strong and to keep thinking that she understands life, its organising principles. She clings to her rigid, protective framework but it is cracking, like an old sea wall that has been leaking for a long time.

My mother realises the power of love when he leaves. My father's love, which she had thought hers, has settled on another woman, another body, and my mother is doubled up in pain and will be for the rest of her life.

My parents loved each other, I know that now. But they suffered from the same wound: their ability to love had been sealed over and undermined for years, since well before they met. Their love was boxed in. Sex was a separate thing, dis-associated from love: a compulsive, substitute act for my father; remote, imposed and impossible for my mother.

My mother loved my father – his sudden fits of joy, his silence, his zest – but she refused his desire and his strength. She wanted a man's tenderness only. Protestant traits were strong within her – a taste for limits and similarities, for smoothing people out, pushing away their desires and differences.

The difference was my father's penis. My mother enjoyed their alikeness but not this big, hard penis, not my father's sturdy body, his pungent smell, his weight on her, pressing down on her silky curves. My mother liked to dance, to whirl around gracefully, but she did not like to be shaken by the desire of a man.

My parents loved each other without saying so, avoiding each other to escape their love without being able to actually leave it behind. They did sometimes help and console each other, furtively and in secret. My father liked the way my mother took care of him. She dressed him, washed him, made sure that his cotton shirts were spotless and well ironed and that he was always served good food and cold beer. But good food was not enough. My father cheated on the wife who refused herself; he would go off but always come back, and she got used to these departures because there was always a return.

At night, my mental merry-go-round kept coming back to

the same question. What is this thing that unites us all? The initial love from which everything follows? That was my question, and when I realised that I had no answer, no clue, when nothing that day had been tender or resembled love, then I would dream of somewhere else that was softer, of flying away, of a land where love would be the focal point of the day, of those films where everything is straightforward and always ends with a kiss so blissful it seems nothing could follow it.

I don't know if there's anything more violent than the refusal, the physical rejection of one's own body by another person. The refusal of its skin, flesh, shape, existence. To be simply denied, held at a distance by a stiff hand or closed lips. That's violent. For my father it was unbearable. It reminded him of being sent away, of boarding school, of his mother's cold, dry hands. My parents were not able to say to each other what I am saying today. They were not able to understand each other, to see each other clearly, to join together love and the body. My parents' love never hatched.

People either emerge from hurt stronger, or they drown. It depends on their nature, and also on luck. My parents drowned, though they pretended to carry on living. My father remarried, my mother never did. I think she waited for my father for the rest of her life, sitting in the living room watching television. I could see that my mother was waiting from the jumpy way she looked up whenever there was a knock at the door, the way her lips gasped apart each time the doorbell rang. The man would come back to her and she would welcome him, take him into her arms, into her body, she would do it for him. She would forgive him everything. She would have thought things through. She would keep loving him, and life without him – those years spent waiting – would have been a bubble, just a bubble that would burst and disappear as soon as my father came back.

I am a divorced child, of divided, uncertain background. Within this division I – supposed fruit of their love – no longer exist. I am sliced in two, separated, fragile. It happened almost forty years ago, yet to me nothing is sadder than my parents' divorce.

22

We return from our holiday sooner than expected. Not to the hotel but to a new apartment my father has bought for us. Everything has been organised, foreseen. We are at the end of a separation process that was begun several months ago. Everything has been planned. Our things and a few bits of furniture have already been moved from the hotel to the apartment. My mother asks to pass by the hotel again. The whore tells her it's not necessary, that everything has been moved. My mother insists – all this is so sudden – and my father ends up saying yes.

My mother has a few hours in which to say goodbye to the place she has managed and held together for fifteen years. She walks from room to room in a daze, her every movement tracked by the new mistress who keeps an eye on her possessions. My mother retrieves a small jewellery box she had hidden under a pile of tablecloths. The contents are checked and my mother is allowed to take away her memories. My mother is calm, strong. In her distress she does, however, forget some basic items. Towels and sheets, such everyday items in a hotel, are left behind. We sleep in sleeping bags for the first few nights. My mother is shocked, driven out, humiliated, but she doesn't falter. I follow her protectively. In defiance I feign indifference. I feel so close to my mother, on the same team for the first time.

On her way out, hurried to the door, my mother puts a hand on the Chinese vase in the lobby, coming to a halt by this familiar object which has witnessed her comings and goings for so many years. She often used to stroke it as she walked past, it was a reference point, she loved its beauty and refinement. She opens her arms, deciding to take it in a fit of bravery; it will be her souvenir, her link, proof that life has not come to an end but is continuing under another roof. Every glance at the vase will recreate the earlier setting and my mother will be able to believe, as she focuses on the magic vessel, that her lonely new life is a temporary hell. Hanny screams, and snatches back the vase.

'That's not yours!'

This woman is simply evil. She wants to hurt, to take revenge. But on what? My mother is not fighting, the battle is not equal. She is emptied while the other is full of venom. I go to take the vase, but my mother holds out her hand to me.

'Come on, let's go . . .'

'Take the vase!'

I look up; my father has been watching the scene from the top of the stairs. He avoids my eyes and returns to his attic.

We don't close the hotel door when we leave.

My mother is holding the vase like a pregnant belly, and my arms are stretched around the jewellery box as if it were plunder.

23

The apartment is a little cramped but we are at home, immovable. My brother and sister argue all day long. Marianne is now a serious, determined, devoted girl. Nicolas is still a roaming kid, his hair has grown and my mother often threatens him with her sewing scissors but can't catch him. My mother is trying to create some semblance of order, to put on a brave face. She has found work. The judge decreed that my mother had no need of maintenance and must work for her living. She does, working hard as is her way, altering clothes in a smart boutique.

'We're a real family now! We're going to eat healthily, and we DO NOT ARGUE!'

My mother hammers out the words to get the attention of Nicolas and Marianne, who are squabbling even as she is making these resolutions. My mother has changed, become softer, warm. She is making a real effort. It's a bit late, but it's nice. 'Better late than never' is her new motto. By repeating these banal words she is trying to get a grip on time and on this wait; she is living in hope.

My mother is bringing us up at last. She is aware we are all she has left and that nothing will change this. She encourages me, telling me I can do anything, that I have the potential to succeed. What? I listen to this sudden promotion. I wonder, and cling to it. It's so different from the old indifference, from what I used to feel, but I try to believe in it. I will need my mother to tell me from morning till night, sober and drunk, happy and unhappy, for every remaining day of her wretched life, that she loves me and that I have talent, the real talent, the talent to be loved, for me to – hearing it so often – start to inhabit this new love, and believe that these words, this change in the air, are more real than what went before.

My mother managed a year of healthy living, without alcohol. She went back to it with the passing time and the never-ending wait. Slowly, gradually, surreptitiously; in a few months she was back to her old levels of consumption. Alcohol and tobacco would be her pastime, her painkillers, till the end.

24

The Mercedes convertible has the top down and is speeding along the school drive. The beast groans, beeps, leaps onto the lawn and skids to a standstill a few yards from Sister Marie Immaculata, who is stiff with fear and fury. A big patch of her short green lawn has just been scalped. Her eyes are dark with unfamiliar anger; gentle Sister Marie looks about to attack in defence of her land.

'It's my father,' I say, ashamed and glad. I have been waiting for him since this morning.

My father jumps out of the speed machine as soon as it stops and walks quickly towards me, holding out his arms. I run up and hug him. Hanny is in the car. Her make-up is a caricature of femininity in which my father thinks he can find an easy, simple life. She must like penetration.

She steps out of the car, avoiding me and cornering Sister Marie, who takes a step back.

'Mother!' shouts the woman.

'Sister!' corrects Marie.

'Sister, I am the new Mrs Kristel, so I'm telling you' – she grabs Sister Marie Immaculata by the arm and leads her away – 'with me, there'll be no more problems! No more drinking! I will be personally overseeing the education of my husband's girls . . .'

My father takes my hand, smiles and leads me towards the car.

Hanny is having an animated discussion with Sister Marie, who is keeping her at a distance by gently pushing her back at regular intervals. My father takes advantage of this to escape for a few minutes, taking me for a short drive. It's Sunday, the spring colours are bright and the air is warm. I lean my head back and let myself be lulled by the regular, mechanical noise of the engine, a noise I have missed. My father is quiet, happy, and I am dreaming away with the top down.

When they've gone Sister Marie Immaculata concludes: 'There's only one thing to do, my girl: pray!'

25

I have come to say goodbye to Sister Marie Immaculata. I've passed my baccalaureate and want to tell her. Unusually, she strokes my cheek, and tells me she knew I would. I talk to her about my plans, because you have to have plans.

'I want to teach, to share . . .'

My voice tapers off; I'm struggling to convince even myself.

'That's good . . .' says Sister Marie, limply.

She doesn't seem convinced either. She knows me well, and knows all about pious hopes, too. But what ought I to do? I'd like to do nothing. Wait for life to paint itself. But that's not possible, you have to have a plan, to make the first brushstroke. Becoming a teacher seems to me easy, obvious, noble. I'll have free time, and hang around with children, remain with them; it'll be joyful, I'll stay like them, I can grow up later.

'How is your mother?'

'Well. We have new rules at home. We're a proper family now. Mum is always saying "Better late than never"!'

'Your mother is wise; that's the definition of hope!'

Sister Marie is surprised at her own philosophical words and soon returns to more practical advice.

'Late is perhaps OK, but not backward. Never be backward!'

Sister Marie makes a quick summary of all she has taught me over the years – guidance on how to live well, to be dignified, to take pride in oneself, to win at life. Then she pauses, and reminds me of the thing she's worrying about: 'Finally, promise me you'll see a doctor if it hasn't come within a year.'

Sister Marie Immaculata is a bit embarrassed, waving at my abdomen.

I am tall but not fully developed. It bothers her.

I promise.

'Right then, run along, my girl!'

Sister Marie hugs me, turns quickly round and walks away. She will smile at other girls, she will carry on. It's summer, a beautiful day. I have my bac, I refuse to be sad.

I still see Sister Marie Immaculata. She's old now but almost unchanged, lovely inside and out. She has remained curious, hungry for life. She has followed my career with interest and circumspection. She has never seen me at the movies, only on television programmes and in the national newspaper *Volkskrant*. She's even cut out a few articles.

She says she always knew that my life would be out of the ordinary.

'You were different. A kind of angel, innocent and impish at the same time. You were keen to learn, I could see your wings growing without knowing where they would take you. You were beautiful, you still are, my girl, graceful, soft and vivacious, funny and sad, different.'

She keeps a few photos of me nearby; she praises my bearing and claims it as her work. She has prayed for me, she says.

26

My body has sprouted but I am not a woman. This suits me fine. I am seventeen years old, with a few baby teeth still. I look as if I'm grown-up. I watch myself in mirrors more and more, playing, angling several mirrors to create infinite reflections of myself. People tell me I'm pretty, and I am establishing whether this is true. What is it to be pretty? My body earns me more and more compliments. People stop me in the street, stare at me, whistle. I am back in the realms of that energy that bound together the men and women in the hotel bar. I feel other people's desire, but not my own. Attracting desire is power over the other, and I discover my power. I am finally the centre of an attention which is strong yet soft, and widespread. It sits on me like silk, never a burden. It warms me then soars up like a kite, with me holding the strings. The connection is there, I will not drop it.

'I don't know anyone who loves themselves as much as you,' my mother often says, intrigued by this egocentric young girl so different to herself.

'I'm not in love with myself, I'm discovering myself. One can't love oneself, one loves other people.'

'Maybe, but I think you're the exception.'

*

I have enrolled at a Protestant teacher training college. The classes hold no interest for me. The disciplines are too many, too diverse and contradictory: literature, maths, history, biology ... my mind is elsewhere. I stare fixedly at the globe that my teachers spin in their hands, travelling in my mind. I meet the eyes of those who gaze at me in class. I examine the beautiful shape of the young woman sitting in front of me, a dead ringer for Greta Garbo. I reply to a boy's insistent stare by dropping my eyes. I am waiting.

27

'But where's the Virgin?' I ask, surprised.

The minister chokes, then scolds me.

'Miss Sylvia Kristel, there is no Holy Virgin, only the mother of Jesus.'

'OK, but where is she?'

'Dear girl, I think you had better learn the basic principles of Protestantism before coming back to this Sunday school. Off you go, please!'

I leave the classroom without a word.

I find the class boring, and the man sad and austere. I need images, need love to be personalised. I like the way Mary is depicted – her pure, slightly sad face, her blue, gold and white robes elegantly draped, her clasped hands, her goodness.

It all seems too abstract without this image, this holy mother. I like the female icon who makes everything seem softer and more serene.

28

My mother is back in her hellish cycle of working and drinking.

She likes her job. She has a new friend, a gentle, supportive woman who will be around for the rest of her life.

Marianne and Nicolas are fighting even more. Marianne grumbles as she cleans him up. Nicolas complains about the food – not enough meat and fish, his growing body needs flesh. It's his way of reproaching my mother for a break-up that none of us can handle. Someone has to pay.

I miss my father. I imagine him as a victim, as weak as he claimed to be. His last words – 'Take the vase!' – were tender, brave, unusual. Perhaps I could help him, try once more to convince him? My mother is going slowly downhill. She has met a Philips salesman, who spends more and more time at our place. He is solitary, kind, and always brings her flowers. But she doesn't want him, she treats him badly, merely accepting the distraction he provides, and the feeling – which she had lost – of being a living being, useful and wanted.

I am growing up, a young woman, rebelling against this other woman whose example I don't wish to follow. I can no longer deal with this situation. I want to cut through it, make it burst. Things must change; so must I. This misery is not for me.

'If you'd had sex a little more often, Dad would have stayed!'

My mother has had a few drinks but she still receives each word like a blow, in silence. My cruelty is a reflection of my suffering. She gulps down the contents of the small glass glued to her fingers and stands up in front of me. I hold my head high, facing her down, not taking back what I have said. She moves towards me, then suddenly stops dead right in front of my face. A warm gust of alcohol and tobacco hits me. My mother is hurt. She clutches my arm, digs her nails into me and shakes me, trying to make me see sense. I resist, still staring into her eyes. Suddenly my mother lets go, yelling, 'Get out! Just get out!'

It's late at night. I leave straight away, I'm out of here, this isn't my life. Where can I sleep tonight? At the home of that nice boy who changes colour as soon as he catches my gaze? No, that just isn't done. At my dad's place! At the hotel, in my room. When I arrive, the first-floor light is on. I can see silhouettes moving. I knock on the reception door and shout: 'Dad! Dad! It's me, Sylvia.'

Sure of myself, looking forward to seeing my dad again. The lights go out one by one. The bedroom is suddenly plunged in darkness, everything completely silent. I wait.

'Dad! It's me! Sylvia! I've seen you! Open up!'

Not a word, not a sign. Nothing. He must be there, she must have warned him, told him not to move, he must be obeying her, weakly. What should I do? My father is there, mute, behind this door he is not going to open. I don't exist. All of a sudden I scream: 'If you don't open the door, I'll kick it down, do you hear me?! I'll kick it down!'

The light goes on. I hear raised voices. Then she comes

down and the two of us talk for a long time. She tries to convince me to leave, for everyone's sake, but I won't. Where would I go?

'If you stay, you'll pay for your room like anyone else.'

'OK.'

The charge for my old room, 21, is a hundred florins. I will work to pay my rent, I can waitress in the exhibition centre. I've watched people serve all my life – my mother, my aunts, the staff. It'll be like second nature, an aptitude gained as a young child, from watching.

My father spends his days in the attic. I see him on Saturdays, when she goes to the hairdresser for a full hour of back-combing. He is happy to see me for this hour a week. If she weren't so obsessed with having a wedding-cake hairstyle to make her look even taller on her hooker's heels, he would never see me alone at all.

I sometimes watch her without her knowing. Trying to understand my father's attraction. It's true that she has a nice body, slim, with shapely female parts. Perhaps that's enough. She dictates and organises everything in a threatening, monotonous voice. Perhaps my father needed to be reprimanded, educated, constrained; men can lose themselves in their freedom.

Everything has changed here. I already knew that. Aunt Alice has been driven out; Hanny claimed she was stealing. One evening she humiliated her.

'Open your bag!'

In it she found a lump of cheese and a little coffee. She convinced my father that Aunt Alice stole frequently and had done so for ages. My father said nothing. Aunt Alice left, mortified.

Aunt Mary flew off the handle, badly this time. She couldn't bear the changes. She put an end to her overly quiet convalescent life, leaving for Italy in an unknown car, with no luggage. She thought she'd escaped. She spent a fortune. Then she came back, saying she had seen paradise, had discovered a country where everything was song and sparkle. She gave herself to one of the locals in a similar fit of enthusiasm. Having thought herself infertile she fell pregnant aged forty. Her rounded belly put a constant smile on her face. Hanny decided to complete my father's isolation by throwing Aunt Mary out on the grounds of immorality. Talk about the pot calling the kettle black – I found out she'd met my father in a seedy bar where she worked as an occasional hostess. By day she was an accountant, by night she hunted for prey – and she wasn't the type to come home empty-handed.

She'd never had a child. Perhaps she couldn't. She hated childhood.

29

I've had enough of Hanny badmouthing my mother, loudly enough to ensure that I'm aware of her daily discrediting campaign and continual bewitching of my dependent father. She walked in on him and me laughing today. It must have been too much for her.

'It's Sylvia or me!' she tells him.

There's talk of placing me with a foster-family.

I phone my mother in tears and she responds: 'Come back, your coffee's waiting.'

She couldn't just say 'I'm waiting'. My mother hid herself behind stock phrases. Her coffee – hot, strong, and always ready – was given as if it came from her own body. It was her attention, her warmth; it was my mother.

I came back, after six months at the hotel.

When my mother opened the door she opened her lips too, giving me a wide, unfamiliar smile.

'I'm glad you're back.'

For me this was an unbelievable discovery; it was evidence, a scrap of love offered at almost eighteen years old, a trigger. My mother's smile restimulated my desire to live my dreams, to take her far away from this grey world, from work and exhaustion.

*

I had blood on my thighs this morning. I was waiting for it, the situation couldn't last. I am a woman. I think of this blood as coming from an invisible wound deep in my belly. I watch it flow, tracing a thick line down my legs. I send a card to Sister Marie Immaculata, who replies by return with several pages expressing her relief and offering advice.

30

I skip classes, if I'm tired or not in the mood. I have a boyfriend, Bernard, very blond and well behaved, with a nice warm smile. His father is a minister. We drink Coca-Cola, smoke roll-ups and explore the texture and wetness of each other's lips; we're always kissing. I feel like a grown-up. In the evenings I wait tables at a restaurant. I earn my pocket money, but without pockets – the rules are strict. Tips are forbidden unless added onto the bill. Our uniforms purposely have no pockets. Some customers regularly leave money on the table, which I have to take back to the till. What a waste! One day I decide to keep hold of this money intended for me and me alone. I fold the notes into four and slip them under my heels. On good evenings my feet barely fit in my shoes. Walking is hard but I do it, proud, thinking of the cash. I tell the customers discreetly but firmly, 'No coins, please!'

I let my mother in on my foot problems.

She laughs and sews a small secret pocket into my dress sleeve, allowing me both comfort and riches.

I help my mother as much as I can. I pay some of our food bill. She is still working hard.

Amazing new televisions are on sale. Colour TV is a revolution in Utrecht. My mother surreptitiously ogles these wonderful machines in the shop windows. They are too expensive, only for the rich – which isn't us these days.

The director of the college calls me in for truancy.

'Miss Kristel, you may deplore the absence of the Virgin Mary in Protestantism, but we deplore your absence pure and simple! Do you have any interest whatsoever in continuing this collaboration of ours? Do you have the slightest excuse for your lack of attendance?'

'No.'

I enrol in an Amsterdam dance school. I have a new boyfriend, Jan, who is affectionate and very handsome. He's a journalist, and drives an Alfa Romeo. People say he's a playboy. Jan encourages me in my new artistic efforts. He thinks me beautiful, as all lovers do.

I love dancing. I am learning graceful new movements for all kinds of rhythms. I am persistent with this discipline, surrendering my body to the required exercises. The music makes me sing and whirl; I feel cheerful, light.

31

I have been sacked from the restaurant. An unfortunate mistake – a sole meunière slipping out of my grasp as I filleted it. I am pleasant and helpful, but easily distracted: 'comely but clumsy!' as Sister Marie Immaculata used to say.

The fish plops with a splash of cream right on the garish skirt of a coarse and uncompromising diner. She screams the usual litany of the angry customer: 'This is unacceptable! Intolerable!' She yells out the price of her skirt. I am sorry. I apologise, grab a clean napkin and bend down to mop up the mess. She pushes me away. When she stands up the fish remains on her skirt, as if grafted on. She is shocked by the beast's tenacity, screams and yanks it off. I laugh. She loses the plot. I am a dolt, nothing but a clumsy lump, a good-for-nothing. The lump gets angry too and is about to add a garnish (the roast potatoes held temptingly in her left hand) when the owner, whom the customer has been screaming for, decides to intervene. He apologises abjectly, holds me back and then takes me away for a chat. It's not the first time, he says. He has already noticed my clumsiness, a trait incompatible with this job.

I am rather sorry. My father had advised me to learn to serve at table in case I might one day take over the management of the hotel. So much for that. I won't be taking our hotel into the next generation.

I slump on the living-room sofa, observing my mother's comings and goings, and her tiredness. I must escape from this back-breaking life. My mother urges me to act.

'How long are you going to sit there doing nothing? "Working hard keeps evil at bay," as your grandmother used to say!'

My mother isn't really joking.

'So, does it work . . . ?'

My mother doesn't say anything. I stand up, kiss her and clear off. I'm going to get a job, make something of my life, buy myself some freedom.

'What on earth are you doing?'

'Keeping evil at bay!'

32

I am hired as a secretary in a metallurgy import-export business.

'Do you even know how to type?' asks my mother.

'Of course! We learned it at boarding school.'

This reassures her.

'Excellent, that's the most important thing . . .'

Actually, it isn't. I am well aware that my boss has employed me not for my secretarial skills, which he never even checked, but for his own enjoyment. For the pleasure of continuing to look at me as he did during the interview, from head to toe and back up again, pausing here and there, his face relaxed and happy. He wasn't listening – I could have replied with the lyrics to a bawdy song and he wouldn't have noticed. It seemed that nothing could distract him from his contemplation. He was not coarse, his gaze was not insistent; he was just charmed. He is a quiet, peaceable man of a certain age.

At the end of my speech, in which I'd outlined my hotel experience, my burgeoning passion for dance, my divorced mother and my excellent English, he asked me to pick up the telephone and introduce myself to an imaginary client. I picked up the handset, said my name like some kind of open sesame and followed it with the name of the company, 'Hello', and a friendly sentence like 'How can I help you?' in a honeyed, rather high-pitched and simpering voice.

'I like you, Miss Kristel,' the boss said. 'You can start whenever you want.'

I made my metallurgy debut the very next day, convinced I would bring a bit of sweetness to that industrial world!

33

'What's your name? Are you part of the line-up? You're so pretty.'

'No, I'm just here with my boyfriend.'

'What a shame . . .'

My cheeks turn red and I look at the floor. The young man walks away, but soon turns round to check if I'm still looking at him. I am intrigued by this charming boy with his lovely wink.

'That's Jacques Charrier, Brigitte Bardot's ex-husband; he's the president of the jury,' explains Jan.

The Utrecht Film Festival is in full swing. New this year is the election of Miss Movies, and Jacques Charrier has devoted himself to the cause. He goes from girl to girl, giving out winks, even stroking some of their cheeks without them flinching. They chuckle softly and tilt their heads. I observe all this. He chose Brigitte Bardot and he thinks me 'so pretty' . . . I am suddenly covered in goosebumps.

'Do you think I'm pretty?'

'Of course,' says Jan candidly.

'As pretty as them?'

'Yes, just as pretty.'

'Very beautiful! The most beautiful of all!' interrupts Jacques Charrier, who has finished his rounds, in English.

I reply: 'You're exaggerating, sir.'

'Believe me, if there's one thing I'm good at, it's recognising female beauty.'

He bursts out laughing, takes me by the arm despite Jan being right there and leads me away.

'May I offer you a drink?'

He is gallant and thoughtful, full of Gallic charm and speaking in English.

'Yes, with pleasure,' I respond in kind.

I tell him all about my little life. I could have been a teacher but it bored me; I am learning dance for my own enjoyment and I work as a secretary to keep my mother happy. In short, I am restless.

'You should be in the movies!'

In the movies? Of course. That's the wonderful job I've been looking for: movie star. Not tiring but fulfilling and pleasant. Perhaps this dreamy girl could make others dream. Jacques Charrier is a producer, he tells me, currently working on a big film called *Closed Shutters* with his friend Jean-Claude Brialy. They are casting at the moment; he would really love me to audition.

'Come to Paris! You must come to Paris!'

'Can I bring my boyfriend?'

'Of course! You'll be my guests, I'll take care of everything!'

'You should be in the movies . . .' The words were murmured, said in English with a French accent; a sweet promise, the thing I was waiting for.

I feel as if I've been invited on my own journey. I am

full of dreams, living in my imaginary world, an innocent, sweet, shiny, loving world. Paris ... the movies ... he believes in me ...

34

My mother silently hands over an envelope addressed to me, bearing the stylish red, white and blue Air France logo. Inside is a return ticket, just one, for Paris, and a little note that says, '*I'm waiting for you.*'

I explain my new professional mission to Jan; he accepts reluctantly.

'You know, those sorts of people promise all kinds of things,' he warns me.

'I can't refuse. It would be rude, don't you think?'

Jan doesn't reply.

My boss encourages me to go to Paris to try my luck. As compensation I'm to tell him all about it, every last detail.

35

Le Bourget. I get out of the plane and pick up the little luggage I have. I walk through the doors, which open for me automatically. I abandon myself to the silently gathered crowd examining every face. I hold my head high and walk slowly. I read the signs bearing all kinds of names, some of them unpronounceable. Mine isn't there. No one is waiting for me. I am disappointed. A new country, a romantic city, I had been looking forward to someone waiting for me, to a meeting; I had been hoping, but can only see unknown faces waiting for someone other than me.

The arrivals lounge empties out. I sit on a metal bench and wait for a short while, before taking some action.

'Ding-dong. M. Charrier expected at Gate C. M. Charrier.'

He arrives eventually, running, out of breath. He kisses me enthusiastically, takes my bag and my hand and starts hurrying out of the terminal.

'Come, come quickly, I'm going to show you Paris!'

There really is a charm particular to the French – a more intense nearness, a tactileness, that flowing language which softens the voice, a gentle chivalry that makes women feel they are the core, the heart of the universe. In my country men are less charming, less patient perhaps, more distant. I am bewitched.

The landscape around the motorway is not pretty. The Mini Cooper is making a hell of a racket. The *périphérique* is grey and monotonous, but then we drive along the Seine and Paris begins to take shape. Jacques regularly attempts to express his affection. He comes closer, each time a little closer, until he is brushing against me, creating in me a yearning for his touch.

The sight of Notre-Dame enchants me. I love its chevets, those elongated projections that call to mind the feet of a spaceship. St-Germain-des-Prés; we're nearly there. The shops are open even though it's after 9 p.m. The streets are crowded, there's a sort of generalised excitement lighting up the mostly young faces. It's alive, merry. We have dinner in an atmospheric restaurant, a lovely vaulted cellar with a jazz orchestra. Jacques sets out the following day's schedule, with one hand on mine and a big happy smile. A 'Barbara' concert, the audition with Jean-Claude Brialy, and an evening with friends. He opens his eyes wide as he says 'friends'. I imagine celebrities, Brigitte Bardot perhaps. My mother won't believe it. We go back to his place, there are two bedrooms, one for him and one for his young son. He puts my bag in his room.

'Make yourself at home!'

I slip obediently into the big bed. He gets in too, very naturally, murmuring a sweet refrain in my ear in French:

'You're so pretty . . .'

Paris thrills me. Jacques is charming, constantly on the move. Barbara has a cello-like voice, bass treble and husky, mysteriously poetic, powerful, breathy: this woman's heart is in her voice, I can hear it. Jacques' friends seem known by the restaurant customers, who come over every now and then to ask for autographs. The few days pass in a whirlwind. One evening I feel tired and decide to go back to the flat early and alone. I stroll around the apartment, looking at the beautiful drawings of studied landscapes and faceless women. I decide to do some myself. I find a piece of blank paper and draw. Then I decide to cook, to make beef and mushrooms for dinner. Certain details leave an indelible memory, I don't know why. Jacques doesn't come home. I leave my untasted dish on the cooker, and go to bed a little sad.

The front door slams, waking me up. It's late. I hear Jacques laughing, he's not alone. I remain in bed for a while then get up, curious. The pretty actress we had dinner with last night is naked in the living room, with the lights off. Her two long, dainty hands are over her pubis. Her dress is on the floor. She is drunk, slow-moving. Jacques is behind her, pushing her gently forward. She takes a step towards the bedroom and slips on the wooden floor, then perches on the back of the sofa, weary of this little journey. She stretches a hand towards me while Jacques strokes her side, from shoulder to hip. I am half asleep, still dreaming perhaps. I shiver, turn away.

'Come here, little sweetheart . . .'

Her tone is soft and velvety. Her voice is faint, but still echoes in the silence. She is lost, and prepared to lose herself further. I am tired, surprised, unsettled. I slip back into the bedroom. Later that night I will notice through the window the young woman fleeing on an unstable bicycle.

'She gets around Paris on her bike; cool, don't you think?'

I don't reply.

'Are you angry?'

'We have bicycles in Holland too, you know.'

I go back to sleep.

There will be no audition with Jean-Claude Brialy. He will simply tell me: 'You are very beautiful, sweetheart, but you'll have to learn French, and perhaps get started in your own country . . .'

I return to Holland as if a treasure has been stolen from me. My step is heavy, I am groggy from these days of excess, my dream plundered.

36

I tell Jan what happened, all of it. I lie as little as possible. It was professional duty, I tell him. Jan is intrigued, and doesn't say anything. Nothing seems to bother him. He is peaceful and linear, just like the life he wants to have with me, and whose mere description sends me running in the other direction. Jan would like a quiet life in a brick house with a little garden bordered with tulips, regular penetration, several smiling children and a guard dog.

My boss interrogates me.

'So, my sweet movie star, how was Paris?'

I tell him how disappointed I was. My stories amuse him.

'You're worth much more than that!' he reassures me. 'You'll see!'

37

My boss is in love with me; he confessed it when he was drunk and I laughed. He sighed, forgave me: 'You're so young.' I continue in my made-up role: docile secretary with a specialist knowledge of metallurgy. I'm not very well informed, but I speak with aplomb. My boss asks me to accompany him on a business trip to America. I gladly accept. He thinks he's got me, but I am merely dreaming of visiting film-star land. Once there, I refuse him straight out, laughing and with a light heart. Annoyed by this, my boss makes himself so ill he is doubled up in pain on the aeroplane.

When we get back to Holland I ask for a few days off, in order to forget the boss's moans as he clamoured to hold my hand in business class, as if it were his last dying wish, begging me to nurse him for his invisible pain.

I take a break. Some intermediary, hibernating time. I return to my beloved idleness, to my mother's sofa: that flat, round-edged little land from which I do not budge. I watch the TV, or my mother, who is reading the paper and glancing impatiently at me from time to time. She can't stand this inertia. Tough. I think about Jan, my boss, the movies, Hollywood and the paths that might lead there. All I saw was Philadelphia.

38

I start actively trying to find this path. My boss has forgiven me. He allows me to take time off work to attend a first audition. I meet Wim Verstappen, a Dutch director freshly lauded for the hugely successful film *Blue Movie*. He is assisted by a young director at the beginning of his career, Pim De La Parra. I take Jan along to the appointment, in order to make things clear. I am looking for a role in a movie and nothing else.

I don't have enough experience. Pim and Wim are charming, and candid. They want to help and advise me to start with a bit of modelling, in order to gain experience with image, light and beautification. Pim gives me contact details for an agency, which I visit immediately. I meet the manager, Corinne, who offers to look after me personally. She believes in me, advises me, moulds me: hair, fittings, a chip-free diet. I am soon called for my first job, photos for a local boutique. It will only take a day and is well paid. I am happy, I'm going to make a slightly better living. Making a living ... Without this mundane necessity, I think I might have spent my life lying on my bed, an imaginary princess, a little sluggish, dreamy, prematurely weary, deaf to the orders of my outraged mother: 'Get out to work!'

*

One gloomy winter evening a few photo sessions later, when I am away from my mother and her ever-present sherry, I surprise her by having a colour television delivered. My mother smiles again, properly, a big smile that lights her up. When I come home a few days later she is still smiling, the smile has been there long enough to culminate in a rare, emphatic kiss, a brief sigh as she holds me close. I feel rewarded, useful and happy, nothing can spoil my joy. My mother's life has been flooded with colours, thanks to me. I will continue to make my living, and so see my mother – my own flesh and blood – smile.

Utrecht station is in sight, on the left. I am walking fast, easily. It's the end of the afternoon and I'm taking the train to Amsterdam. I have a booking at the agency. It's an important booking, a national campaign for *Elle* magazine. If it goes according to plan my face will be all over the country. I smile at my nymphs. To my right, the hotel looks the same as ever. My attic window is a small angular box among the sloping tiles. It was from that tiny space that I dreamed of flying away. I look away from the hotel, back in the right direction: straight ahead. A man sitting on a bench is staring at me, slowly turning his head to follow my progress. I look at him and smile; he seems pleasant and peaceful. He must be fairly old, about my dad's age perhaps. He has a long brown beard and very pale eyes, he is playing the flute and looks like some kind of dropout. I walk out of his field of vision and his neck gets stuck at the end of its rotation. I turn round, laughing openly at this transient fascination.

'Miss! Miss! Wait! Wait!'

I hold my head high and pick up my pace. What if he's a 'crook'? Sister Marie Immaculata used to say that the devil wore a benign mask. The man stands up and heads in my direction. I speed up again. He catches up with me and taps my shoulder.

'Honestly! What do you want?'

'Nothing bad. I feel blown away and I wanted to thank you.'

'Whatever for?'

'For that moment.'

'Thank you, you're very kind, but –'

'You're an angel! An indefinable alloy –'

Amazing, him using that metallurgical term.

'Listen, sir,' I interrupt him, 'I have a train to catch, I must dash, please excuse me.'

'Give me your hand.'

'Really!'

'Give me your hand, I say.'

The man's voice has become so warm that I hold out my hand.

'The right, your right hand, please.'

He seizes the hand I have proffered like a princess; seizes it gently, then turns it over and brings my palm right up close to his eyes.

'Your life will be intense. You are very talented. You will be better known than Sophia Loren!'

I look down, take back my hand, rush off. I'm going to miss the train.

39

'It's a big contract, you see, the campaign will be in *Elle* magazine, in Holland and Belgium. The photo shoot is planned for next week, at the coast. You'll have to be free for three whole days.'

'I can't. It's the metallurgy conference.'

'Listen,' says Corinne, 'this contract is worth six months of your salary, or even more if it's reused. For three days' posing – think about it . . .'

'I want to be in the movies.'

Corinne is taken aback, and replies: 'That's a good idea, it could happen, but one thing at a time. You're young, you've plenty of time. You could be in the movies in a few years, when you're less in demand for photos.'

'I want to be in the movies! As soon as possible; I want to be an actress.'

'Come on, not straight away!'

'I want to be an actress.'

Corinne doesn't reply, just looks in her notebook for a name and number, which she gives to me.

'Phone Elly Claus, she's a friend of mine, a casting director; she'll see you.'

I grab the piece of paper nervously, folding it so many times that it becomes a small soft pebble held in my clenched fist like a winning ticket.

40

Kees is a funny and outrageous head stylist I meet on a shoot. He waves his hands around when he talks as if he were onstage. He is bisexual, he says. I'm not really sure what this new concept means. Bi must be better than mono, like having an extra talent. We flirt, we have a lot of fun together. I introduce Kees to Jan, my blond playboy. They like each other straight away, drawn together like magnets. I will lose them both, developing my understanding of bisexuality through this concrete example.

I am suddenly alone, not really sad, just latent, once more flopping around on my mother's sofa. I think of 'Uncle' Hans and his red-coated lover. I am pensive and indolent; my mother hates seeing me in this state.

'You should enter!'

My mother's loud words make me jump.

The television addict stands up and holds out an advert she has circled in the newspaper: 'BECOME MISS TV HOLLAND!' My mother is right, I must get moving again.

I send off a photo. They contact me. I will be interviewed by four people and must convince them of how much I want to be a TV presenter. I think of how thrilled my mother would be to see me on her magic box, and feel as if I could talk forever. Before I go in an assistant advises me to show off my legs, crossing them slightly to one side. At that time legs were important; TV presenters were offered to the public in their totality. I hitch my skirt up slightly. People say I have nice legs. I hold them together like a little mermaid, crossing them daintily at the ankles. I smile and speak softly. I am called back.

My picture appears in the newspaper every day, alongside those of my ten competitors. The eleven Dutch provinces are represented. It's a bit like a livestock contest: spot the regional difference. I am doubtful. How? The paleness of the complexion, the curve of the cheek, the shape of the eyes? Some are more rustic than others, all are pretty, the differences are in our expressions. My mother is amused, and rather proud. She says I don't look like any of them, that I resemble none of the regional variants. I was right, the idea of seeing her daughter on television every day absolutely thrills her. It seems that to interest my mother I must be far away – at boarding school or on screen.

The winner will be elected by the readers of the paper, over the course of several weeks.

I've won! By a long way, I'm told. A tidy sum of money, completely unexpected, that leaves my mother speechless. I have an appointment with a TV boss for my first screen tests.

This success delights me. I was chosen, voted for . . . at work, my colleagues congratulate me. My boss grumbles, saying: 'Television will suit you better than secretarial work!'

I take his advice and resign.

I've found the tiny piece of folded paper bearing the number for Elly Claus, the casting director. I postpone my appointment with the TV people and call Elly, strong and proud of my new title.

'Hello, I am Miss TV Holland and I would like to be in the movies.'

'Well, that's a first! And what does a Miss TV Holland look like?'

She laughs at my nerve and invites me to meet her in Amsterdam.

41

'Come in, Miss TV Holland!'

'Hello, Mrs Claus.'

The apartment is big, with high ceilings, white walls, modern art paintings, occasional cheerful splashes of colour and a white grand piano. I immediately adore this harmonious, fresh space. She's a beautiful woman, feminine and fully made up. Her movements are graceful, sweeping, her hair is soft and blonde. She's Anita Ekberg and this is the movies. At the end of her long slim fingers burn long slim cigarettes. Inhaling the smoke with weary ritual, lips pursed, she declares with a curling motion of her hand: 'You're not at all like I imagined. Your voice is so soft. I thought you would be blonde, with long hair and nice rosy cheeks! The popular, familiar type of look that has already been seen everywhere. You know, like those girls on TV presenting the weather as they wiggle their hips in front of posters of tulips.'

'I don't understand.'

'You're pretty.'

She examines me from every angle, gently lifting my chin.

'Your eyes, your mouth, your neck are delicate. What colour are your eyes?'

'It depends . . .'

'On what, the weather, Miss TV Holland?'

'No, on my mood.'

She comes up close, pulls her lips into a grin just above my nose and looks deep into my eyes with her white-hot gaze.

No woman has ever been so close to me.

Her lips are so near. I can smell her breath, the menthol scent of her mouth with that familiar backdrop of warm tobacco.

She smells of compost, of mint-flavoured mildewed forest leaves. Is she going to kiss me, to reproduce a kiss from the movies? I close my eyes, protecting my mouth with a slight retreat.

I would like her to pull away as well, back off. I wish gently for this, without moving any further away myself. If a kiss is needed, I will do it. My heart is beating, my stomach churning. Elly blows her earthy breath over my cheeks. I have been granted a pardon.

'What part of town do you live in?'

'I live in Utrecht.'

'Utrecht! What a pain! That's a city for learning, not sparkling! It's important to have a bit of fun, life goes by so quick . . .'

She comes back towards me and strokes my face.

'Do you smoke?'

'Yes, but only filterless cigarettes.'

'Filterless? How dreadful, how can you inhale those exhaust fumes?'

She moves away.

I am fascinated. She sits back down and tells me to do the same. She tells me all about her life, about the famous husband from whom she is separated, Hugo Claus, a well-known Belgian author and the father of her son. She had been very beautiful in her youth, Salvador Dali himself begged her to pose ... Then she interrupts herself:

'You must come to Amsterdam! I will help you find somewhere to live. I'm sure Hugo could take you in.'

I will make my movie debut thanks to Elly; our fascination is mutual. The film is called *Because of the Cats* and is directed by Fons Rademakers. I play the leader of a small gang of rebellious girls called 'The Cats'. It's rather violent, a less bitter *Clockwork Orange*. My part is small but the film is an international production. Alexandra Stewart remembers me, we'd met in Paris just a few months ago. She is amused by the coincidence and gives me a spontaneous hug. The director vaunts my beauty, comments on how natural I am. I feel flattered. I am more convinced about my naturalness than my beauty. It's true that I'm at ease in this new chaos, this busyness, the technicians milling around, the attention on me.

When the camera comes up close to my face I find that I can see myself in it as in a mirror. I look at my precise, slightly enlarged reflection, the velvet of my skin, my neither sad nor happy look; a familiar, friendly reflection.

'It's a small part. I'd like a starring role!'

Elly laughs.

'You're so greedy!'

I need to leave Utrecht. Elly gives me her husband's address. Hugo Claus owns a building and lets out apartments.

'Go and see him, tell him I sent you. He'll like you ...'

Elly bites her lip, sighs deeply and turns her head away in a little cloud of smoke that veils her troubled face.

42

The capital is where it all happens, I'm sure of that. The big smoke, where I've got to be, at the heart of things, where everything intersects. The lovely city of Amsterdam. Hugo Claus owns a whole five-storey edifice divided into two semi-detached properties. Numbers 5 and 7 Raamgracht Street. I like the area. It's a mixture of all the places I have known, urban life at the end of a street bisected by the canal, surrounded by water, bordered by trees. It feels like being in the country. Sundayish, grandmotherly. At the top of the building is a triangular white cornice like a hat, concealing two intertwined angels sitting on a bed of corn; it's charming, absolutely charming. A big white baroque church steeple stands tall behind them – the Southern Church, like the turret of a naive chateau. At the top a gold weathervane shines in the sun. The winter is bright and clear; I look up, high, towards the sun. I love the rooftops, the views, the perched statues. I want to grab hold of the steeple's weathervane, to examine up close with my short-sighted eyes what those angels are doing. It seems that humans have been more inspired by the upper reaches of the world than its base; that goes for me, too.

The church bell rings every half-hour, and tolls out the hours. A veritable concert of bells serves as my clock, forcing me to be on time, both thrilling and annoying me. The mechanical, incessant beating of time.

I like freedom, and constraint. I recognise myself in both, and can move easily from one to the other. I like to submit, and also to make others submit. It isn't contradictory, just how things are, how I am. I like to have boundaries because they were lacking for me, and I like freedom because it was she who brought me up. Freedom is in my nature. I am a free woman who likes constraint, or the opposite. I am made of this mixture. This conflict shaped my life, and ruined it too, made and messed it up to leave me finally, as in the wake of war, with a sense of balance and peace. I developed between two extremes, overcoming contradiction to create my own harmony, shaping my own blurred personality, mixing my own colour just as gold and blue make green, the green of this water in the little Raamgracht canal.

Hugo Claus is a charming, impressive, steady, still man. His face is as lined as the bark of a tree. He has a big nose and reminds me of a gentle ogre. He seems solid and the skin of his hands calls to mind the hide of an animal. He welcomes me pleasantly and shows me my apartment, polite and a little distant, respecting my great youth. There are twenty-four years between us. I call my mother, who is worrying as if I were out on my own for the first time. She tells me an intriguing letter has arrived from England.

'Well, open it!'

She reads, enunciating the foreign words slowly, her accent rough: '"Miss TV Europe"? Miss TV Europe! You've been selected for the Miss TV Europe competition!'

43

We're going to London. All expenses paid. We're taking the plane. Mum has organised everything. She is laden with enough luggage for a military expedition. She has filled a make-up box with a huge range of colours. 'You've got to look your best!' Her little leather sewing box is full to bursting. My evening dress, which she has so skilfully made, ironed and folded, takes up a whole suitcase. Mum puts it in the locker above our heads.

My mother's excitement is at its peak. For me all this is almost to be expected, a logical progression.

My mother elbows me, whispering in my ear: 'Have you seen who's sitting on your right?'

I turn round immediately. Another poke.

'Don't be so obvious, Sylvia!'

It's a Dutch TV presenter, absolutely the most famous, meaning that to my mother he's a living god. He smiles at me and says a few friendly words. I tell him our story. Amused by the coincidence, he tells me that he's on the Miss TV Europe jury. My mother keeps up her pokes, bouncing up and down in her chair.

'Sylvia, it's a sign!' she whispers.

'You'll vote for me, won't you?'

'I'd love to, but we're not allowed to vote for our own country.'

'Well, cheat then!'

He grins, and carries on talking to me. I introduce the restless, bubbling-over creature to my left. He stretches out a gallant hand. My mother falters, blushes with a nervous fluttering of the eyes, and nearly faints.

44

London. The Churchill Hotel is very smart. My mother inspects the room as a fellow professional, impressed, murmuring, as she examines the pleats of the curtains: 'It's like a palace. This competition of yours is so well organised. They're treating you superbly, you know . . .'

The bathroom is made from pale grey marble which my mother strokes with a tenderness I have never seen. I decide to run a luxurious bubble bath, pouring in one of the dainty, sweet-smelling little bottles. My legs will soon be emerging long and slim from the bubbles, as with my steaming, outstretched hand I hold a glass of gently fizzing champagne, thinking how sweet life can be.

No holding my breath, no games; I'll keep my hair nice and dry, clipped up above my neck, which will lie comfortably on the inflatable cushion.

A sparkling necklace and the scene in my head would be perfectly reproduced. I look for the champagne.

'Champagne?! But it costs extra!'

My mother wants to bring me back down to earth.

I don't reply, just keep looking.

'Aren't you going to revise?'

My mother has brought me books on London, its history,

what happens here ... and another on Holland since the barbarian invasions.

'Mum, it's not a competition for teachers, it's a TV programme. I've just got to be the prettiest and the most entertaining. I'm bound to get their attention, and succeed. I'll do my little show and it will be dazzling. The judges will vote for me, they will see only me. This is my moment, my big moment. I'm going to be a star.'

'A star? ...'

My mother thinks quietly to herself. Stars are American, or Italian or French, but not Dutch. It's a question of nature, and of culture. We are not an extravagant, egocentric nation; we are industrious, shrewd, disciplined – the most sober of the monarchies. A down-to-earth people, somewhat lacking land, occasionally travelling the seas to conquer more but certainly not dreaming of being stars. My mother believes in me, tells me I am very talented, but being a star is quite another matter. She says she can't think of a Dutch person since Van Gogh who is known beyond our borders. My chances are slim.

'You'll see, Mum. I'll be a star, it'll be my profession!'

'But it's not a profession!'

'It'll be mine.'

I stop listening. I take off my clothes and fold them neatly. I cover my nakedness with a soft, embroidered towelling bathrobe. In the entrance way are doors for stylish built-in wardrobes. I open them and discover to my delight a small windowless room with subdued lighting, pale wood drawers and hangers stamped with the hotel's name.

'It's called a dressing room!' cries my mother over the sound of the television, which she has on loud – a habit she has kept since my father, lying next to her, used to complain that he couldn't hear it.

It occurs to me that there's enough space in this 'dressing room' for my mother to have a pleasant stay in it.

I've found the champagne! My mother sighs. I confidently pull out the ice-cold bottle stashed in a little fridge under the TV.

'That's called a minibar!' says my mother, continuing her guided tour. 'At least make do with the half-bottle. Don't get done like some customers, who drink the whole bloody lot thinking it's on the house!'

I glance at the prices on the pretty little menu, but don't understand pounds and can't be bothered to do any mental arithmetic. I fill two flutes to the brim and put the bottle back in the fridge. My mother accepts the one I pass her, eyes glued to the screen. I walk slowly to the bathroom, from which a slow, dense current of steam is already escaping. My mother turns her head and looks at me. I am more compelling than the television. I'm walking across the room as if on a tightrope. Pretending to be on a catwalk, playing. My thighs rub gently against each other, my hips sway and tilt, I put one arm around the back of my waist and with the other I drink, chin held high to catch the light of the chandelier, profile perfect. I walk with pride and confidence, bearing an invisible crown, and enter my hot, humid heaven as a queen enters her kingdom. My mother bursts out laughing. I slam the door.

The water is scalding, my heart a crazy tambourine, my sweat running down in big droplets. I drink, delicately pouring the still-cold champagne into my hot mouth. The mirror is covered in a thick coat of steam. Water is rolling down it in great streams which I scrutinise from very close up, as one does with insects. I glue my nose to the mirror, watching the condensed steam flow down, watching the droplets form. I can see only a blurred image of myself on this ruined mirror, striped by the streams of water. I write my name in capital letters on the steam with a squealing finger, and then apply my mouth to a still-virgin space beneath the fading letters. I push my soft lips into the glass, then detach them. An impression remains, showing each crease of my lips. I rub it out with my elbow, laughing. I rub out my name, wipe off all the steam to make the mirror reflective again and see my mother's horrified face behind me. She is shaking her head and saying softly: 'My dear girl, I don't know anyone who loves themselves as much as you do . . .'

Her serious tone makes me laugh.

'I've already told you that's not true. I don't love myself, I'm finding myself, looking at myself close up, I can only see close up.'

45

The show is presented live by the well-known Katie Boyle. We are asked to arrive a few hours early, to rehearse our entrances and responses one last time. We have spent the week filming little London scenes: Sylvia next to Big Ben, Sylvia at the National Gallery in front of Van Gogh's *Irises*, Sylvia on the shoulders of a Formula 1 driver, Sylvia stretched out exhausted on the bed. My mother has had a brilliant week. They've organised a special programme for the families and she's taken to it like a duck to water. She can speak English, which surprises me. She says she learned it speaking to the foreign customers at the hotel. When she can't think of an English word she just says the Dutch one, confidently and in her best accent. She claims she already knows London like the back of her hand, and sees the television presenter from the plane almost every day. In the evenings my mother regales me with tales of her day. She seems happy.

Katie Boyle is very sweet, protective and funny, with her hair in curlers before we go out live. We fall into line, like at boarding school, and Katie looks over her troops. She stops in front of me and murmurs: 'You're very pretty, Miss Holland . . .'

I look down without replying; a shiver runs down my spine, making my shoulders tremble. I can feel the other girls looking at me, a swarm of Miss Vengefuls ready to disfigure me just before we go on air. But in fact these international Misses are very well behaved, white with fear, mute. The cameras don't intimidate me, or the projectors, I'm already familiar with them and in any case can only see the closest ones.

'In a few minutes this empty room will be filled with a noisy, spontaneous crowd. Don't let yourselves be overawed, stay focused, the crowd is on your side.'

I am not overawed, just impatient. I'm waiting for the crowd, for the moment when – perhaps – it will choose me. There would be no point in this whole performance without the audience. The crowd will elect me, like a sweet, obedient nation. I've been looking at myself alone for a long time, making faces, singing, dancing and waving my arms around – all alone. I've been waiting a long time.

My mother is in the room, very nervous of course. I think of her and smile, imagining her proud and dazzled enough for two. During the break she comes to find me in the wings, as jumpy as a flea. Her words are tumbling over each other in the most unfamiliar way. She has just realised I've a real chance of winning, and she's all over the place.

'You're the prettiest, the most natural, the most graceful. You're the only one!' She stops, then starts again: 'Miss England is pretty too, but she can't win with a name like that!'

My mother is right. Zoë Spink is very beautiful, a little gentle for my taste but with a dazzling, frank smile. Here she is in her own country, with her own audience, her fellow countrymen: the judges are bound to be susceptible to this shouting, biased crowd. I shiver. How unfair if Zoë Spink were to win because she's English and we're in England. Suddenly I'm no longer sure, my intuitive confidence sinks like a lead balloon. The importance of what's at stake sweeps over me. My heart is hammering. I know that winning would change my life. I want to win, to be recognised, for my life to change, and my mother's life too. I want my father to see me, to see this exquisite bird he allowed to escape. I want Hanny to choke on her own hate, Aunt Mary to sing as she waves frantically at the screen, my sister to jump up and down screaming that I am indeed her sister.

This is a boiling desire, and it moves me. I am nothing but a child, about to act the fool just as I did in the hotel bar, spinning around on my bike and being clapped and congratulated. People will say my name in voices full of joy, warm voices; they will announce this result which will ring in the start of my party. I will be happy. I will play, and I will be chosen; I will be borne, through others, into the dazzling light.

It's time. A fire bell sounds, we fall into line backstage and the funny, crazily enthusiastic voice of Katie Boyle rings out then disappears under clapping so thunderous it makes me breathless. The crowd is there, roaring like a monster. The racket is surreal, unexpected, much louder than the attic din I used to flee, a terrifying, human, massive and exciting noise.

'Thank you! Thank you so much!'

Katie thanks the crazed, starved crowd, and calls us onto the stage.

We walk on in single file. The Misses smile widely, a little frantically, baring each of their teeth as if exhibiting merchandise. I opt for a shy, reserved little smile, a promise, a forebear of hidden treasures. We are each holding a small banner announcing our country. I would have liked to add a personal message, such as 'HOLLAND: SECOND HOME TO THE STARS', but then I'd rather have people see that in my face, my body.

The group events are the easiest, we sashay along in near-synchronised movements, turning right at the end of the stage to avoid falling off like lemmings. We walk towards the crowd then pivot, our individual flourishes slowly dispersing this delightful procession of spangled nymphets.

I have refused to pose on fake sand in a ridiculous swimming costume in the depths of the London winter. It is very hot under the spotlights, however. I've chosen to wear a short little skirt and tights, with a flowery blouse and a dainty sun hat: beachwear with a twist.

Time for the individual event. I am changing clothes, about to slip on the dress my mother has made. An orange-tinged pale red silk.

'To go with your hair!' she'd assured me. 'They look wonderful together!'

My hair is auburn, a lovely shiny copper, but my mother seems to be the only one who thinks my hair and this dress go well together. The dresser just looks puzzled.

'Interesting colour.'

'My dress is very beautiful; my mother made it.'

I no longer have time for uncertainty. The dresser hands me my clothes robotically, one at a time.

'No, no bra!' I tell her.

The dresser protests, uncomprehending. She seems to be saying (in very rapid English) that this would be bad form, not done, too shocking. I don't give a damn. I know what I want.

She's still holding the unwanted bra; she drops it limply and sits down. I have destroyed the dresser, my first victim. I laugh and dress myself, alone and happy.

It's my turn. I walk onto the stage, ridding my mind of any doubts. Who will believe in me if I don't? My mother, perhaps. The crowd claps and I clap too, nervously. I walk towards the blinding spotlights on the floor in front of me. I can't see the crowd. I think of my mother, I know she's there, I can feel her; it's as if I can hear her inimitable voice carrying me.

'So, lovely Sylvia, what do you do?'

'I'm a film actress. I've just made a big film in Holland, I had the lead role. I'm interested in ... literature. I love reading, Hugo Claus is a friend of mine. He's delightful ...'

I speak in a confident but gentle voice, sweeping the horizon with my gaze.

'And now you're going to dance, is that right?'

'Yes.'

'To a tune well suited to your country! "Tiptoe Through the Tulips"! Over to you, Sylvia!'

The crowd applauds.

Over to me! The tune is hardly original – I didn't choose it – but never mind, I'm going to transform it. I know how to dance, I've taken lessons. I hear Sister Marie Immaculata's voice in my head: 'Stand tall! Hold your head high! It's not what's on the ground that's nigh!'

I dance an English waltz. I am light, dignified, upright and smiling, my arms almost straight, at a courtly distance from my partner, who is examining my curves, the movement of my legs under my dress, and my breasts doing their own waltz, undulating beneath the silk.

The music comes to an end, the crowd claps, they are still clapping.

I take a bow, curtsy gracefully and leave the stage.

I give, yet keep them wanting.

Zoë Spink is the final performer.

'So, lovely Zoë, what do you do in your spare time?'

'I like ponies,' she replies, in a soft little voice.

The crowd laughs, and so does Katie Boyle. Zoë blushes vividly.

The judges deliberate.

Ponies? What a strange reply, the language of a little girl. I hum *'Cream-coloured ponies, crisp apple strudels . . .'*, trying to get the better of my nerves, waiting.

So here I am, a few yards away from a jury which may hold the keys to my liberation, waiting just behind a curtain which hasn't yet opened.

'And the winner is . . .'

I shut my eyes, breathe in deeply and carry on singing this hymn to my sister and to childhood, softly, just for myself . . . *'When the dog bites, when the bee stings . . . these are a few of my favourite things . . .'*

Katie Boyle strikes up a different tune, with a broad smile:

'Tiptoe through the tulips . . .'

I have beaten Miss England by just four points, four points which will change the course of my life. I feel sure that if Zoë Spink had said 'horse riding' instead of 'ponies', with the confidence needed to bring out the nobility of that activity, she would have won, would instead have beaten me by a few points. One word, and life takes a different road, changing everything irreversibly.

Katie Boyle hugs me as the crowd roars and trembles. An endless, delicious noise that gives me goosebumps. I blow kisses beyond the wall of lights to the back of the room, walking up to the spotlights, right near the jury and the audience. I'm trying to see my mother, I would like to see my mother.

People are fussing around me. Covering me, wrapping me up like a beautiful gift. A white ermine coat, a pretty crown with very sparkling, very fake jewels, my hair being stroked, strangers kissing me, shouting compliments, all this attention, all this sudden, sparkling and unreal attention . . .

'We can die now, Mum!'

I fling myself at my mother, who has found me and is crying and jumping up and down at the same time. The waiting, the hoping and now success make her much more effusive than usual. The show is over, but mine is just beginning. The pace is hotting up, the fervour is palpable, my mother is getting excited.

'Die? You're so lazy! Let's live! This is just the beginning!'

The next day Mum is up early. She carefully cuts out every news article and photo of the television show she took part in, and which led to the little crowning of her big daughter. My mother is in one of the photos, with a simple caption that she reads out again and again: 'MISS TV EUROPE AND HER MOTHER.' Mum is dazzled, knocked out. Her dull life has been suddenly swept away and her memories effaced for a while by this unexpected, delightful time of joy. She has bought a stack of newspapers, and is starting the scrapbook she will continue for almost thirty years.

Success is like a wind blowing in, a source of constant

change. I've stepped onto a fast-moving carousel which carries me effortlessly along.

A telegram from the Dutch Prime Minister. My mother reads it out, so moved she stumbles over every word. There are flowers everywhere. People keep ringing at the door. A press attaché gives me my schedule for the day, already harried at the thought of what is to come. The chief administrative officer arrives to tell me more about each of the many prizes I have won. Each participating country has given me a designer wardrobe. Mercedes-Benz is giving me an 'S' grade limousine, and there's a holiday in Jamaica from an airline company. Then a substantial cheque is presented to me as my mother looks on open-mouthed, sitting down, more stunned than me by this whirlwind.

I negotiate with Mercedes to give me cash instead of the car. My savings are growing.

Back in Amsterdam, I walk triumphantly into my bank to make a deposit and a transfer to my mother.

The fashion agency congratulates me – I've already received messages and post, and there's a note from Elly asking to see me. Everybody wants to see me, they've all got plans for me.

At home, even the great writer Hugo Claus congratulates me, amused to have a 'European tenant', as he says. He watched the show and thought me 'very beautiful, ethereal, sparkling'. Ethereal? His eyes light up; I look down.

'Thank you very much.'

I am fascinated by this older man. A man who initially didn't seem to see me, but is now discovering me – whereas I watched him from the very first moment. His body is huge, his features pronounced. His eyes shine with a calm fire, a desire that burns, that goes beyond me, wanting more than just me. The desire to live intensely, to take advantage of every possible opportunity, to enrich one's life with numerous impulses and actions, with creativity, with thought.

This handsome man seems to be constantly turning things over in his mind, and his serenity comes from this process of thought. His desire is intense, and controlled.

That's what it is; I don't feel his desire for me because he is controlling it, calming it. I am going to stir him up. I like this man, like him hugely, infinitely. I like his control, his reassuring body.

I take the plunge, unable to help myself.

'I'm going to the movies tonight; would you care to accompany me?'

I am trying to speak properly.

He smiles, barely surprised.

'Gladly.'

'Wonderful. I'll ring at your door at seven.'

The film isn't very good. I knew it wouldn't be. I wanted to make sure my landlord wasn't too captivated, that he didn't forget me. He is sitting next to me, impassive. I shift around, change position, fidget impatiently. My guest pretends to be indifferent, watching what I'm up to out of the corner of his eye. I can bear it no longer.

'Would you mind terribly kissing me?!'

He didn't mind. Hugo kissed me slowly, tenderly, fully. Without a word. His tanned, soft hands brushed against me, warmed my cheeks, gently lifted my chin. Held so lovingly, so precisely, floating on unknown waters, I felt myself become precious.

I changed rooms, shared his bed, the warmth of his body and a part of his life.

Hugo likes my candour, my youth, my cheekiness and that radiance which lights up small stars more brightly than great writers. Because they embody a common dream – people dream of being a star, of being young, beautiful, rich, free, unique, loved. I was. I stirred people's dreams.

46

Hugo is the father I would like to have had, and the lover I've always dreamed of. A father-lover. A subtle, powerful, yearned-for blend, at the far reaches of desire, immensely, shamefully resonant, at the edge of love, way beyond reality. A perfect, attentive, indulgent father, who teaches me things. Right here, by my side, an adult, a controlled, polite, self-made man, a lover whose body is as strong as his mind. An aware, gentle, generous, big-hearted adult, made of fire and ice. Hugo is my life. We are inseparable.

The difference between us entertains Hugo, he enjoys himself with me. He's a vibrant forty-something; his energy is youthful but his body seems to have lived longer than his years. He has wisdom, the reserve of the old but the madness and freedom of the child. His childhood has stayed so close it has never left him. Childhood is not a reference point somewhere back in time, it is him; he is a function of his childhood. He bears the deep scars of emotions experienced too young. His body is thick and coarse, the robust envelope for a precious, tender heart. Hugo has been watching and feeling for a long time. He dissects people, life, the movement of life, and keeps every image meticulously noted and classified in his enormous mind – a treasure trove which, when opened, spurts forth diverse and luminous expression. Precise, unusual words which, when put together, create a soft, bewitching music, a familiar tune, the pure song of the wounded child.

Hugo had a wretched childhood.

His life began alone, sent away at eighteen months old. Tiny, alone, not realising his aloneness because he knew nothing else. An almost innate solitude that at first built him up and protected him, but after the event ruined him, as he grew older and started discovering that life could have been otherwise.

Hugo's father also created books. He was a printer, he made them physically. What a team they could have made – the form and the substance. But Hugo hated his father. He took up boxing to defend himself in a fight which occurred only in his head and heart.

Hugo has written of solitude, its anger and pain – as if it were past – as well as the wild, wonderful desire to live. Hugo has scoured the roots of pain: *The Sorrow of Belgium*, his best book, is his own story.

There's something to be said for a wretched childhood. That precocious experience of suffering, when combined with a fertile nature produces almost limitless bursts of creativity, fireworks of original colours. Pain is a part of art. Artists need to be loved.

Hugo kept himself thoroughly entertained. He made the most of life and its pleasures – he was a father, a husband several times over, an artist and businessman, and very much a lover. He tried everything. For a few years Hugo was mine.

I keep Hugo exquisitely entertained. He hangs out with a group of intellectuals – as described by themselves and others. They use a lot of long words, and laugh at ordinary ones. They seem to understand and recognise each other. They are always thinking. They intimidate me, of course, and they like that. They are the intellectuals and I play the pretty one: those are our roles. They are a little jealous, and don't really think much of me. I entertain them, too – which is all a Miss TV Europe could hope to do – and I am attractive, the people's goddess. Sometimes I notice their desire (not so intellectual now) and read the physical urges of their bodies. They get on my nerves, so I provoke them and hit the bullseye – the body triumphs over the mind every time.

'I can't take you anywhere!' Hugo says to me, affectionately.

'Why can't you? If only *intellectuals* were allowed out, the streets would be so sad! They'd be empty!'

I make Hugo laugh. My understanding of life and of men is considerable, as is my impact. I may seem a little gauche but I'm just keeping my well-honed cards close to my chest.

I am young, slightly famous, people recognise me in the street and I like it. There's something vital in this impulse of other people towards me, like an end in itself, a caress. I've seen intellectuals perish from a lack of recognition and caress. I've met more egotists than intellectuals, each of them searching for the most effective way to act interesting and obtain love.

You can't take me anywhere? Maybe, but I'm so much fun that flamboyant, teasing, loving, contradictory Hugo ends up taking me everywhere. He shows me off in a rather unintellectual display of male pride, displaying through me the righteous variety of his nature, his appetite for the simple life, for the physical, for me. We go to all the restaurants, the nightclubs, all the fashionable places.

He gallantly walks in first, then puts me in the spotlight. He likes other people's eyes on me, that collective attention he never quite garners. He likes people's frivolity, this mass impulse that carries its own truth.

Hugo is a fount of knowledge. His learning is huge: literature, history, philosophy, mythology ... he loves telling me about those fascinating gods from times past, divine archetypes in a superhuman theatre.

He tells me I'm a 'modern muse' – not a reproduction but something new.

Elly came round to Raamgracht Street. She burst in like a tornado and said to me: 'You, little girl, are going to let the grown-ups talk among themselves!' Hugo sent her away politely and calmly, reminding her that if he paid her so dearly it was so he could live in peace. She left, hopeless and sad. I was shocked. I saw in this defeated, suddenly lustreless woman the fate that perhaps awaited me. Hugo asked me to stay where I was, in his apartment.

Elly wanted Hugo back, more than anything. She hid her obsession behind composure and perfect grooming. This ravishing, wonderfully vibrant woman had men falling at her feet but she wanted only one, the man who had rejected her. This rejection was her obsession. Elly couldn't bear it that Hugo no longer loved her. But did he love at all?

Hugo is an exceptional person, extremely hard to get over.

I received something funny in the post today. My old boss from the metallurgy company had seen a photo in the papers of Hugo Claus, aged forty-four, accompanied by the lovely young Miss TV Europe, aged twenty, and had taken offence at

Hôtel du Commerce, opposite the central station in Utrecht.

Grandmother Kristel.

Uncle Hans.

With Aunt Mary and Max.

Reading *Donald Duck*.

My parents.

My mother with her
faithful suitor.

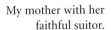

Miss TV Europe competition, 1973 (front row, third from right).

With Hugo Claus.

From *Emmanuelle*.

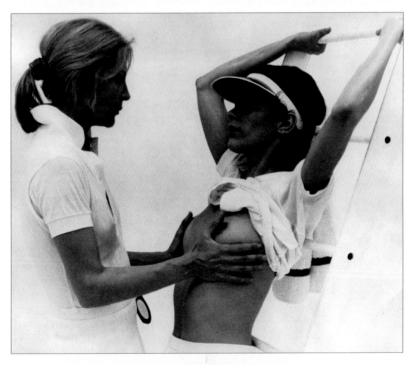

With Jeanne Colletin in *Emmanuelle*.

With Marika Green
in *Emmanuelle*.

Photographed by
Francis Giacobetti
for *Lui* magazine.

At the Cannes
Film Festival, 1975.

From *René la Canne*
with Gérard
Depardieu, 1977.

With Ian McShane at home
in Los Angeles, 1978.

With Arthur in LA, 1978.

With Freddy de Vree
in Santa Monica.

At the Karlovy Vary Film Festival in 2003
with Wim Verstappen (left) and Freddy de
Vree (right). Bessel Kok stands second from
right and Martina Kok third from right.

With Arthur.

the age difference, which I had always used as
put off his advances. My boss could have been n
He was in love, and blind. I replied to him sweetly
just how it is, you don't choose who you fall in lo
that I had wonderful memories of my time as his se
wished him and his company all the happiness and
in the world.

47

Elly has put me in two more films: *Living Apart Together* by my first mentor Pim De La Parra, whom I'm delighted to see again, and *Naked Over the Fence* by Fras Weisz, in which I play a singer.

During the final days on set I receive a call from a casting agent friend I met on my first film. She congratulates me teasingly on my European win: she'd found me very beautiful, different, arousing, and a good actress. She tells me about a casting that's happening right now, something very particular that I absolutely must try for. An unusual film, very erotic. She insists that it is not at all vulgar; the director, whom she has met, has a strong artistic sensibility. The film is inspired by a novel, and it's a French production. The director is called Just Jaeckin, this is his first film, but he is already known in the world of fashion photography for his strong aesthetic sense. The producer wants to create a big splash – the first erotic film for the general public. It's an important, seminal role.

The book is *Emmanuelle* by Emmanuelle Arsan. An autobiographical novel, not just erotic but pornographic. In it everything is explicit. The body, penetration, the erogenous zones, their movement. The cover sets the tone: apple-shaped curvaceous buttocks, with a serpent twirled around them like a spiral of peeled skin.

From *Private Lessons* with Eric Brown, 1981.

From *Lady Chatterley's Lover* with Nicholas Clay, 1981.

Painting in Ramatuelle, France, 1989.

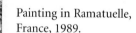

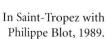

In Saint-Tropez with Philippe Blot, 1989.

Hugo knows the book.

'The novel is interesting, but if the film is anything like the book it'll never get past the censors!'

When the book came out – at the end of the sixties though it was clandestinely published in 1957 – it was well received by the critics. André Breton said it was very well written. I read it long after the casting, once I'd accepted the role. The text was daring, blunt; it described a shameless, unfamiliar, initiatory sexuality that would have put me off. I had a feeling it might. I was dreaming of a strong role without knowing the details; dreams don't bother with details. I wanted a seminal film, a springboard which would make me a worldwide name and fling wide the door to the movies and the life of my dreams.

I decide to attend the casting. No well-known French actress will touch it: they all say it's pornography, which is already widespread, shown through a network of badly lit specialist cinemas that smell of fresh sperm and stale air.

I know that in my hands the role of Emmanuelle will never be reduced to pornography. I know this intuitively. Hugo's remark about the potential censorship of the film provokes in me a strong reaction to the contrary, an electric determination, a taste for controversy and subtle rebellion. Will I be able to marry my morality and strict education with my taste for excess? No actress wants this role? Fine, I'll do it myself, and better than anyone. I will be the Emmanuelle they are looking for. I will dissolve into their desire, I'll become someone else, I will act.

I am warned that I'll have to undress for the casting – at least my top half. That seems fair enough for an erotic role. Although, actually, I'm quite prudish, and uncomfortable with nudity. To understand my modesty you must first understand the extent of my need, my desire to be looked at and loved.

As a child at the hotel I used to dance naked – during the day with Marianne, and alone on the roof at night, when the moon was full and bright. That wasn't an immodest act, it was a call:

The summer heat wave was keeping me awake. An insomniac, cognac-filled little girl watching the moon. The station nymphs were smiling at me and I was dreaming ...

I look up at the sky, seeing in that giant cameo the face of a religious woman weeping with her head bent. The moon is full and perfectly round. It is luring me, I am hopping and fidgeting around ... I am going to climb through the window onto the roof. Marianne is sleeping, her face peaceful. I put out my finger to touch her cheek, breathing in the tobacco aroma that has emanated from her since she's been spending her time at the neighbours' house. If she doesn't move at the touch of my fingers she is deeply asleep; that's my signal, I can leave. I open both sides of the window, haul myself up onto the radiator, grab hold of the lintel and put a first foot in the gutter. I clutch the concrete ledge above the window and move along the tiled roof, suspended, my arms stretched taut. I get round the window and climb onto the square platform. My stage. I straighten up and dance, whirling around, at my own secret ball. I love the night, it's more fun than the day, I feel freer and life, temporarily slowed down, seems kinder. A few stunned passers-by see me up there in the bright moonlight. They point. I sit down so I can no longer be seen and they walk on. I dance some more, in the light of the moon, laughing, taking off my clothes, shouting a little ... I dance in the warm air, naked.

My nudity in films is a casting against type. I have never cured myself of my prudishness, just dressed and hidden it, and lied. As I've taken off my clothes I've created the pretence of naturalness, of a second nature behind my good education and bourgeois bearing. In my attempt to convince others, I have almost managed to convince myself.

48

I go to the audition. How will they ask me to undress? I am dreading harsh words, a vulgar zealousness that will shock me, a crass order I will refuse, so I decide to beat them to it. I will take off my clothes before I'm even asked. I'll avoid the awkwardness; I'll invent before their astonished eyes my second nature, my taste for nudity. I will be confident, charming and utterly headstrong.

I am wearing a lingerie-type dress with delicate shoulder straps; it reaches halfway down my thighs.

I sit down and smile. I'm twenty years old with all the nerve of that age, all the desire to conquer.

Yes, I have been in movies already, and want to be a professional actress. Yes, I love France, and travelling. Yes, I know how to ride a horse, and can speak several languages. Yes to everything.

I take advantage of a boring question about my education to roll my shoulder slowly forward until one strap falls, and then the other. I carry on talking. The slightly cold air stiffens my breasts, making me very aware of my nudity in front of this fully dressed audience. My clear diction is unaltered by my sudden wilful movement. My apparent relaxation and indifference give the impression that my body is still dressed although it is right here, in front of them, exposed, naked. The panel is bowled over; some of them even have the tips of their tongues hanging out . . .

The questions stop. I laugh and ask: 'Will that be all?'

'Yes, that's perfect, we'll be in touch. Thank you.'

Time goes by, a month, two months. Jaeckin is hesitating. He shows the scriptwriter Jean-Louis Richard all the screen tests and Jean-Louis points to me, saying: 'That's the one!'

Jaeckin calls me to Paris for a photo shoot, to check. Hugo comes with me, which impresses them. Jaeckin is neither literary nor intellectual. I meet the other actresses, Jeanne Colletin from the Comédie-Française, Marika Green from the underground scene and Christine Boisson, a teenager just starting out. We find ourselves standing there with our breasts on display as if at a trade fair for women; joyful, consenting women. The part of the older man, my mentor in the film, will be played by the great Alain Cuny, who starred in Marcel Carné's *The Devil's Envoys*. Jean-Louis Richard is a well-respected scriptwriter who often works for François Truffaut. I feel sure that such an excellent team is bound to make a good film.

The producer Yves Rousset-Rouard makes the decision in the end. He likes my physique, and as much as my body my bearing, my voice, a certain elegance and distinction. Emmanuelle's world is one of privilege; the eroticism must be stylised. The unusual, discordant nature of my relationship with Hugo is attractive – Yves can already sense the press interest there's bound to be in this 'golden couple', the nymphet and the intellectual.

*

I will be Emmanuelle. It's confirmed. The producer is enthusiastic and ambitious, he's dreaming of a bigger success than *Last Tango in Paris*. I am delighted. But the most difficult thing – my mother's blessing – is still to obtain. I am afraid of her reaction. More than afraid, paralysed. Only she can put an end to this dream. I will not hurt my mother. If she winces or objects I will go back on my contract.

'Mum! I've been given a starring role! I'm going to be in an extraordinary French film.'

'But that's fantastic!'

'Yes, but it's a very . . . liberated film.'

'Liberated from what?'

My mother doesn't understand.

'It's a film that breaks taboos . . . a modern film . . . a very beautiful story. I will be naked, Mum.'

My mother stops speaking, contemplates my enthusiasm and the fire behind my fear, and then smiles.

'If you think this film will be good for you, then do it. But don't ask me to watch it.'

I have been chosen and my mother has agreed. I savour my victory. I have resounding proof of my own determination and others' desire for me, and the promise of a new life. Hugo congratulates me. He keeps saying that the book is strong, daring. He is curious as to how it will be adapted.

That evening, in the bathroom, I clean myself. I take a long shower, feeling the hot, abundant water stream over my body. I relax, let myself dream. I look at my body in the mirror, and for the first time see it as a tool. I look at this winning figure, and wonder. I examine it. I want to know, to find the formula for their benediction. Apart from the 'elegance', this body must

From *Private Lessons* with Eric Brown, 1981.

From *Lady Chatterley's Lover* with Nicholas Clay, 1981.

Painting in Ramatuelle, France, 1989.

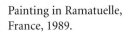

In Saint-Tropez with Philippe Blot, 1989.

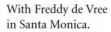

With Freddy de Vree
in Santa Monica.

At the Karlovy Vary Film Festival in 2003
with Wim Verstappen (left) and Freddy de
Vree (right). Bessel Kok stands second from
right and Martina Kok third from right.

With Arthur.

47

Elly has put me in two more films: *Living Apart Together* by my first mentor Pim De La Parra, whom I'm delighted to see again, and *Naked Over the Fence* by Fras Weisz, in which I play a singer.

During the final days on set I receive a call from a casting agent friend I met on my first film. She congratulates me teasingly on my European win: she'd found me very beautiful, different, arousing, and a good actress. She tells me about a casting that's happening right now, something very particular that I absolutely must try for. An unusual film, very erotic. She insists that it is not at all vulgar; the director, whom she has met, has a strong artistic sensibility. The film is inspired by a novel, and it's a French production. The director is called Just Jaeckin, this is his first film, but he is already known in the world of fashion photography for his strong aesthetic sense. The producer wants to create a big splash – the first erotic film for the general public. It's an important, seminal role.

The book is *Emmanuelle* by Emmanuelle Arsan. An autobiographical novel, not just erotic but pornographic. In it everything is explicit. The body, penetration, the erogenous zones, their movement. The cover sets the tone: apple-shaped curvaceous buttocks, with a serpent twirled around them like a spiral of peeled skin.

the age difference, which I had always used as an argument to put off his advances. My boss could have been my grandfather. He was in love, and blind. I replied to him sweetly, saying that's just how it is, you don't choose who you fall in love with, and that I had wonderful memories of my time as his secretary and wished him and his company all the happiness and prosperity in the world.

hold clues, reasons, an explication for this keen desire, this choice.

The basin is set low and the line of light bulbs reminds me of a theatre dressing room. I dry myself gently and methodically, limb by limb. The sight of the whole reveals nothing new. I look myself over from head to foot. My eyes are the part I know best, I look at them again, their colour is still indefinite, changeable, sea green, grey, yellow, ringed with anthracite. In them I see fire, and absence. They can burn, darken or mist over with a pastel tone. My hair is short and not terribly feminine. My nose is straight, slightly turned up at the end, small and classic, as standard as a doll's nose. My lips are open and fleshy, especially the bottom one, which stands out the most. It is the recipient of kisses, and seems to tremble. At the edge of my smile is a milk tooth, smaller and off-white, the sign of unfinished growth. My shoulders are narrow, rounded and well cast. My breasts are nicely shaped, pale, regular, modest without being small, intact. If children had breasts they would be like mine. My hips are a woman's hips, wide and protruding. On tiptoe I can see the tops of my thighs, my pubis; I stop there. I have found a few clues, yet I'm undefined, a mixture; simultaneously woman, girl and boy. An artless face – my smooth, neutral mask for a gaping heart, and sometimes, in my hot, furtive eyes, fever and rage.

I convince myself that the beauty of the lighting and sets will be like a veil over my body.

My modesty will be obvious, my gaze elsewhere. My expression will clothe me. I will be caressed without caressing in return. Each movement of my body will portray my aloofness and distance. Beneath the closed eyes of ecstasy will be born an unreal, intimate world of fantasy. On-screen I will be untouchable, unfathomable, theoretical; I will send out contradictory messages, creating a fertile, unsettling, vast space in which every person, every memory, every desire will find its place.

Hugo knows my duality, my complexity, my modesty. He understands these clashes that live within me in contrived harmony. He likes this alloy. He says that I will give the role a unique and fresh resonance.

Thailand for a few months – not a film but an extended holiday. The country wasn't then what it is today. At that time the countryside was full of never-seen, intensely lush and luxuriant landscapes.

It is the dry season and yet the strangely shaped leaves are saturated with water. The colours of the flowers are bold and vivid. The plants gleam, as if made of plastic. Nature here is generous, rampant, wild, powerful, unique.

Our hotel is in a remote part of Chiang Mai. The walls are made of white wood. It's an old, light, elegant colonial building, open to the wind, to movement, to the surrounding countryside. At night I hear unfamiliar cries, which Hugo tells me are birds. Strange kinds of birds that scream in the middle of the night like newborn babies or the about-to-be-killed. I find the countryside much more frightening than the city. Each time I hear one of these cries I start and cuddle up closer to Hugo.

'You're ridiculous . . .' he says tenderly.

I try to sleep under the fan. The huge propeller turns slowly, a never-ending spiral at which I stare for hours.

Hugo has come with me. My man has followed me, he is my reference point, my support, my security. With him by my side I can do anything.

Emmanuelle Arsan has refused to meet me. She doesn't understand the producer's choice; I am nothing like her character. She is the heroine of her own book, it's her story. She is Eurasian, dark-haired, short, an emancipated woman before her time. I am tall, pale, docile, with strict morals, shaped by my religious education. She comments that Emmanuelle would never have brought her partner to the set. She would have devoured the crew and the natives with contagious nymphomania. Not me. I behave as if married – faithful and conventional. My real desires are not sexual.

I have never made love in front of anyone, or with strangers, or women, or made love all the time, senselessly, as if physical love and orgasm were the immediate and sole purpose of life. I have made love, not often. My desire is weak, recent and passive. I am curious, loving, I want to please rather than to come.

'I hate penetration! I hate penetration! . . .'

My mother's words ring in my head like echoes in a closed room. Those words have atrophied my desire, almost sealed it in for good. I am not sure that my mother was telling the truth. She was unhappy, and frightened. Afraid of unknown, forbidden pleasure, of inexplicable desire, of bodily strength, afraid that my father loved her only for that reason, so he could penetrate her.

When Hugo's desire brings mine to life, like a bud, my fear evaporates. For a moment, this rare moment, I abandon myself to carnal contact. I find it silky, as soft as my mother's words were vicious, as tender as my 'uncle' Hans's tongue was manic, hurried, murderous.

I become petted, penetrated, loved. I take in this friendly penis, letting it slip right into me. My flesh becomes wet and sticky. We are inside each other, a single, blended, dynamic, allied, complete sex, the same living body. Right until the final groan I hear the man and woman crying rather than moaning. Solitude is broken by this wonderful union. No longer being alone, becoming dependent, touches me. It's not sex that should be forbidden, but loneliness.

In these rare, protected, loved moments, I like penetration.

Hugo reassures me, talks to me, keeps telling me that the erotic aspect of the part doesn't bother him. It's the movies, he doesn't mind, on the contrary it entertains and titillates him.

An enormous, never-expressed fear overwhelms me just before the first scene. I am standing up, frozen, my eyes closed. For a fraction of a second my arms become rigid, I can hardly breathe, I'm slipping. I've overestimated my strength, I'm just a little lost kid from Utrecht, totally out of my depth. This is a mistake, it's no good, not me, I don't want to play any more. I am shaking, about to faint. The grown-up, confident, ambitious girl has evaporated into the tropical heat. I think of my mother, my grandmother, the newspaper she stuck on the mirror to hide my reflection. My childhood fears attack me. I think of everything that should be hidden and forgotten and that I am about to show, recklessly, as a result of blind arrogance and destructive desires.

My will is stronger than my fear.

I breathe, and open my eyes. I walk forward. I smile. Action!

As soon as I hear that word I will become a replica of myself, gracious and determined, but aloof.

The first scene is a normal scene with Marika. Then comes the caress, and then the kiss. Kissing is easy. No. It's an eminently intimate, exclusive act, a promise that moves me deeply. Touching the tip of my beloved's tongue with my tongue creates soft electricity all over my skin and in the depths of my belly.

For the first time I will kiss without desire, a mechanical but not symbolic act. My first kiss will mark the beginning of my cinematic isolation. To allow my body to accomplish this, to accept the kiss of this unknown person I will cut myself off, and enter a dreamland. My body may be working but my dreams remain free and invisible, like those shrieking birds. And in this isolation, this ticket out, everything will become possible.

Moaning, stroking, licking, faking the pleasure I have not yet found. A stranger carries me to an aeroplane toilet and takes me immediately, rocking me on the toilet seat. He grips my open thighs, my head falls back, I am submissive, offered up. I groan, he comes. I will, with great naturalness, do everything I need to do to satisfy the director, and the ambitious producer. I will be professional, absolutely professional and punctual, organised. I will repeat my movements. I will place those little square bits of sponge neatly over my pubis. This methodical approach will help me forget some of what this is about, the immodesty, the seediness, eroticism for sale. I will fake it convincingly. This role, so opposite to what I really am, will be my best role, the hardest, a real achievement, completely made up, an illusion, a dream. I am an actress.

'You might move a little, you're like a dead fish!'

Hugo means well with his blunt responses to the rushes.

A dead fish? I don't laugh. A fish, a faceless animal? Am I inexpressive? Have I overdone the aloofness? Does Hugo want me to give the world what I am trying to keep for him? I will not move more, other actresses do that already, shrieking and fucking hysterically. Not me, not here. It will be my trademark, the proof of my difference, of the subtle effort I'm making that one day I will be able to discuss, analyse, explain. I will remain detached, rather still, demonstrating my control. I will give myself but I won't be there. They will never have me, will keep on wanting me, trawling for me, I am a big fish.

49

'Daniel! Let me explain it to you! Your wife is returning home after a long time away, you want her, you abandon yourself, letting her do what she wants with you. You sit on the edge of the bed, already bare-chested, and then lie down slowly. It's a slow, voluptuous surrender. You, Sylvia, when Daniel sits down on the bed, you sit on top of him and, when he goes to lie down, you kiss him as if you wanted to hold him upright with your lips. Then you realise what he wants, you anticipate his desire. You move down his chest slowly, covering it with little kisses, slipping down towards his groin. See what I mean?'

'Yes . . .'

I ask for a little champagne, a glass which I down in one, and another for good measure. I smile. The groin it is. The wife of my screen husband Daniel Sarky is on-set; she cannot hide her nerves and nor can Daniel. He is sweating, struggling with this incongruous presence. It might be the movies but it's still my skin, my lips, my breasts.

Action! I can't remember my lines. There aren't many – I have to suggestively ask my husband whether he's missed me – but I can't remember the exact words. I stop the scene at the point where Daniel goes to lie down.

'I'm sorry, I can't remember my lines.'

'Don't stop the scene for that, love. You'll be dubbed anyway, remember. It won't be your voice. Keep moving your lips and if you can't remember, it doesn't matter. Say whatever you want in any language you like, just keep moving your lips.'

Jaeckin means to be reassuring, but I am devastated. My head is spinning. I like the script, the words sound right, they flow, they are mysterious, erotic, at least as erotic as us. Moving my lips whatever the language is ridiculous. I have to slip down his belly, the scene is risqué, no one gives a damn about the words. I know I will be dubbed, that my accent is still rough, that Emmanuelle is a real Montmartre Frenchwoman. But I want to speak, to express myself, to prove that I understand.

This role I had imagined as a springboard shrank me for good. My body was more interesting than my words. Taking away my speech was like cutting off one of my senses. I was celebrated for my body, for a piece of me, a chosen piece but a piece all the same. I was a mute movie star, truncated, deprived of the entirety which constitutes a human being.

My 'talking' roles never worked. They may be far more numerous than my 'silent' parts but they've been forgotten, rejected. It wasn't up to me. I was a voiceless, pigeonholed actress. I belonged to the realm of dreams, to that which cannot be shattered.

The champagne flows and I forget. I obey; things will change, one day I'll be heard. I move my lips, hide my baby tooth, lie down, roll around in the sheets, go for it; I don't give a damn. Daniel makes hygienic love to me, in fits and starts between

'Action!' and 'Cut!' His excitement is fairly well controlled, under his wife's attentive gaze.

I suddenly burst into fits of giggles. This situation is grotesque. Two hours in a bed with a kind, handsome work colleague, as nervous and drenched as a female fountain, humping away with our official partners sitting a few inches from the bed. Hugo amused, not jealous, Daniel's wife captivated, disconcerted, astounded by this upmarket peep show. Once her surprise has passed she will become impatient, but Daniel will still be sweating. When the scene is done, I hear a relieved sigh from the wife. She borrows Hugo's copy of the script, which she seems to be reading for the first time. How far will this go? Will she be able to bear it? Wisely, she decides to leave the shoot.

Today I have to masturbate. Yesterday I watched them shoot a scene in which two women masturbated each other. They were local women, nightclub dancers, sex professionals.

Today it's my turn. I ask for a cigarette, I've run out. They search the whole set; no filterless cigarettes. They bring me a hand-rolled cigarette in a copper bowl.

'That's kind. What is it?'

'Thai cigarette, Miss! Very good!'

Wonderful, thank you. I ask for a short break while I smoke this traditional cigarette. I'm surprised by its unusual taste. Everything here is exotic, that's for sure. The finished cigarette is in the ashtray, and I have left the building. Jaeckin's impatient face comes in and out of focus. Hugo's voice is far away, slow and deep, ghostly. The manicure is over; my hands, which will be shown in close-up, look lovely, but my nails are growing before my very eyes! I feel good, free, as if I'm in a cartoon. Everything looks rounder, brighter, and rather wobbly. It all seems softer, innocent, amusing.

'Sylvia? Sylvia! Time's up! Sylvia?'

Sylvia doesn't move from her seat. When my name is called I find I can't reply. Why should I? What's so important? I let them talk, the words hum gently around me, I laugh, I close my eyes and laugh.

'What has she taken?!'

'Thai stick! Thai stick!'

Hand-rolled local grass. I am completely out of it, and spend the rest of the day in a parallel universe. Drip-fed coffee and gently but repeatedly slapped around the face, my heart hammering. My eyes have rolled up in my face. I will finally masturbate the next day, very grateful for the remains of that fog.

At the film screening in England I burst out laughing when we get to that scene. It's so obvious that my unfocused eyes are more drugged than feverish! This nervous laugh is also an expression of discomfort. I feel the immodesty of that scene more vividly because it resembles me more – that solitary act in which nothing is shared, that stubborn quest for physical pleasure.

My Thai stick has thrown the whole crew behind schedule. I acquire their forgiveness by throwing a little party at the hotel.

Today, I will be raped. I hate this scene. The violence, the physical constraint makes me want to run away. My partner isn't a professional actor, he's a handsome young native chosen for his chiselled body. He doesn't seem to understand what's going on. He is bare-chested, wearing a loincloth. The scene takes place in a smoking den. It's one of the final stages of the initiatory journey into which Alain Cluny urges me. Opium suffuses the air. The boy is standing about, having a great time already. Jaeckin is communicating with his hands, showing him how he must move, miming the feel of the scene. Emmanuelle refuses this violent act but her greedy body accepts it.

My partner nods his head in a sign of bewildered approval. His empty eyes worry me.

'He hasn't understood the scene!' I say. 'This isn't OK!'

'Don't get upset, it's a simple scene, he's understood fine. This is the movies, love. Let's do it!'

I have to wriggle around like a fresh fish, turning my head every which way without really struggling. I am ready. I'm wearing a Balenciaga dress in pearl-grey silk – embellished with pleated flounces – that shows off my naked back, and two pairs of knickers! My partner and two burly boys emerge from the shadows. I notice three cameras, instead of one. The scene promises to be as spectacular and unrepeatable as an avalanche, so they need to cover every angle. The penetrating man sweats above me. The two others hold my arms down. I find the position unbearable but I keep quiet.

'Action!'

The young rapist rips off the clothes fettering him and pounces on me as if going into battle. He grasps hold of my waist and pushes up my dress. He pulls down my undies and pushes his hard penis against my closed body. I scream, I'm suffocating, I push this man off me with a strength he wasn't expecting. I yank my hands away from the others. I'm crying, screaming, 'Cut! Stop! Stop!'

I refuse to redo the scene immediately. The interpreter is

absent today and I insist that he's replaced – Jaeckin's mimed explanations are not explicit enough. It will take me a long time to get over that awful experience. I have them repeat over and over to this simple man that this is not real, it's acting, cinema. I may be naked and lying down, but that's because I'm posing, giving myself as if to a painter. I'm giving myself to the film, not to him.

He doesn't seem to understand anything . . . or am I simply afraid? An irrepressible, ancient terror. I grasp hold of his shoulders – I'm taller than him – I shout in French: 'Gently! OK? Gently!' He sees the anger in my eyes and understands. When it is over I leave immediately.

My dress is destroyed, my lovely dress, the nicest, most scene-stealing dress I wear in the entire film. I am shocked.

The budget is so tight that we have very few outfits and they are counting the rolls of film. We often use the first take, and the crew double up as extras. It's fun. They don't warn me, and then in a small crowd scene – a garden party, perhaps – my husband introduces me to the producer or the sound engineer, or the make-up artist, and I have to say: 'How lovely to meet you.' I smile, the situation is funny and unexpected. The atmosphere on-set improves.

Money is scarce but the team is strong. The cameraman is Robert Fraisse, who will be nominated for an Oscar many years later for his cinematography in Jean-Jacques Annaud's *The Lover*. Photography director Richard Suzuki does a careful job, lighting me well. Watching the rushes I notice the golden mellowness of his work, and after that I seek it out, basking in it. Lighting for an actress is like the sun, essential; all the more so when you're naked. The light dresses me.

The critical and public reaction focused on the lesbian scenes, and how at ease I seemed in them. But that wasn't something I was used to. Their questions aimed to delve into the nature of my actual sexuality. Emmanuelle's ability to take pleasure wherever she finds it, regardless of gender, troubles men and women who aren't as free. They want a clear picture, when these things are far from black and white. They want to categorise my sexuality, to identify me, to reduce me even further. I refuse to reply to these intrusive and simplistic questions, skirting playfully around them. I allow arousal and desire to live, without giving it a shape. I stand surety for Emmanuelle and her freedom. I joke around, saying that women's skin is softer, as familiar to me as my own, that my fears evaporate when touching a woman, that I'm reassured by this gender complicity, by women's basic tenderness, by our similarity.

The erotic scenes follow one after the other, and I get used to it. In this country where sexuality is widely commercialised but strictly regulated, the producer has managed to obtain the permission of an influential prince to shoot nude scenes in wild but accessible places usually deprived of such lust.

The mood is pleasant as filming continues. Hugo has hit it off with Alain Cuny – they hold forth about Baudelaire while I continue my exploits with the help of champagne and Thai stick.

In a fit of venality the producer has decided he wants a shocking scene, one that will attract as much attention as the infamous scene in *Last Tango in Paris.* He's concerned that all this will be a little tame and insipid.

In the Bangkok clubs, women perform horribly degrading acts with their vaginas. The ultimate holiday souvenir, what a stroke of good luck! The tourist can choose – ping-pong ball or cigarette? The producer is a smoker. Ever the aesthete, Jaeckin rejects this opportunistic scene which could topple the film into ugly and absurd pornography. The producer insists.

The cameraman will shoot the scene. A young girl is chosen. She will smoke through her vagina, doubled over with her face invisible. The scene is despicable, apparently; I've never seen it. I've only watched the English version, in which this scene was cut as a result of censorship or simple good taste. In the countries such as France in which the scene was kept, it didn't meet the producer's aim. 'The Scene' was rarely mentioned, and has in fact been forgotten.

The film encounters its first disaster. Jaeckin wants my husband to drive a yellow E-type Jaguar for the scene of my arrival in town. Not only actresses have whims! We eventually find the only available model in the whole country. An entertaining tulip-coloured sports car with a huge bonnet and two ridiculous seats. The thing is proudly and immaculately polished between each take by the millionaire owner's chauffeur.

'It is worth a lot of money?' I ask, curiously.

'A fortune! As much as the film's whole budget!' jokes the producer, who has forbidden anyone to come near the car.

This phenomenon is driven far too fast by my fiery husband, and crumples in two on a rocky hillock after an impressive flight through the air. I am a stupefied onlooker to the scene. The producer chokes with rage and likewise loses control, showering Daniel, the reckless, groggy, confused driver, with insults. Daniel blames the power of the car. The Jaguar is not insured, we're going to run out of money, it's all over. If Daniel didn't still have a few scenes to shoot I think Yves would have resorted to his fists!

Jaeckin likes freedom, he's an artist, creative, he wants a change of scene. On one of his walks he has come across a superb waterfall, its sheer abundance suggestive. This spurting, frothy water has inspired him, it's full of 'good vibrations'. The crew follows him, migrating to a new land. Marika and I start up our naive, chortling water-nymph act on discovery of this rural setting that resembles us in its wild purity.

The good vibrations don't last long. We're all arrested by uniformed police. To start with I think it's a practical joke, then a very realistic improvised scene, with extras in perfect costumes. But no, this is a brutal return to reality; the water nymphs are taken to the police station in our dressing gowns.

Jaeckin, the devilish instigator, is thrown in prison. The police want to confiscate the film. The shrewd cameraman had already hidden it, and gives them a bit of virgin roll instead. We'd been trespassing on private land without permission. A monk had come up to the waterfall brandishing wet earth in an upheld hand, he had shouted, no one had understood him or even recognised him from his outfit, and he had been thrown off the set. We were on sacred land and the monk had reported our unspeakable desecration to the authorities.

We are accused of immorality. These helmeted Thais are yelling ferociously. I want to leave, I'm barely dressed, I've had enough of this joke now. I decide to find out whether my powers of seduction work on this side of the globe . . .

'Dear sirs, I need to go back to the waterfall, I've left my sandal behind!' I am smiling, pouting and batting my eyes.

The reply is immediately translated: 'If you don't shut your mouth, you'll never see another sandal in your life!'

Then the men start yelling again, and the interpreter refuses to translate another word. He apologises, and explains in polished French that the policemen are spewing offensive insults. I wonder what ... whore? slut? Those would be the first insults aimed at me. I remain calm, friendly, docile; I look down, fold inwards, protect myself by pulling my dressing gown as close around me as possible. I want to disappear. Jaeckin is questioned incessantly and made to give his personal particulars to the bombastic, omnipotent officers over and over again. The country has undergone a 180-degree shift, from idyllic setting to rigid, anarchic seat of hypocritical repression. I feel completely unsafe. I'm afraid, though I don't show it. Immorality? It's true, all this *is* immoral. I will be arrested, judged, imprisoned, and they will be right.

But the producer has more than one ace to his pack. He has friends at the embassy and he also contacts the prince. They agree to let us go for an unofficial ransom. Money will buy us freedom.

The prince suggests we continue the film in his Bangkok studios. A traumatised Jaeckin gladly accepts.

We leave after a final outdoor scene, a scene I've been dreading since the beginning. I know I won't be able to do it. I am tense – horse riding is for me even more perilous than unbridled eroticism. Yes, I lied. I have never ridden a horse. And? I wasn't going to miss out on *Emmanuelle* for a few seconds trotting through the rice fields. Jaeckin sulks, the producer shouts. What were they expecting? Lascivious contortions at the gallop? They'd envisioned a close-up but we settle for a long shot. I remind them that in *Viva Maria!* Brigitte Bardot filmed on a fake horse. They don't give a damn. Photography director Richard Suzuki has short hair like me and is the only crew member who can ride, so he will put on my lovely spring dress and ride the beast through the setting sun, making sure to keep his back to the camera. He will have all my moral support, all my attention from afar, and I will keep the guilty fits of laughter to myself.

We've almost reached the end, which is a problem. Jaeckin doesn't know how to bring the film to a close. How do you end a story that was never a story to start with? What photo do you choose for the end of an album? An extra scene? A different, unexpected scene? Another shocker? They decide that I will make love with two men. This will be a symbol of Emmanuelle's emancipation, her maturity, her definitive abandon to an endless, guiltless lust ... I agree to the scene, presented by Jaeckin as a metaphysical success. It will be implied, quick, dreamlike. I agree in order to get this over with.

The very last scene is a self-portrait. I am free to do whatever I want. The camera freezes on my face. I wind a feather boa – the showgirl's talisman, the loose girl's plumage – around my neck, and shadow my eyes in thick black kohl. They are in mourning.

'Mourning for your lost youth!' says Jaeckin the philosopher. 'Emmanuelle has grown up!'

No. My dreams are what I've lost.

*

My favourite scene is the one in the swimming pool. It was shot twice, because Jaeckin wasn't satisfied. First in Thailand and then near Paris, at Le Vesinet.

It's February, and silver birches have replaced the palm trees. Jaeckin dives into the icy water, driven by unconscious, infectious enthusiasm. I follow him after a cognac, warmed by alcohol and the fever to please, to make lovely images. Christine Boisson is more hesitant, calling us 'nutcases'. She will experience fever too, but the real kind: Christine will catch a severe and long-lasting pneumonia.

I open my eyes underwater and see nothing but that intense clarity you get high up and in great cold. In the winter the surface of the water is as smooth as a gently lapping silver tablecloth. I can do whatever I want. This is my free time, where I get to express myself. I tack and turn, my legs kicking, my russet pubic hair waving in the water like algae. I sink and then wind my way back up, dancing, living, cleansing myself in this clear water. I exhale little bubbles that rise up towards the air. I follow them. I take another breath and dive back down. I am not cold, I believe that.

Hugo is watching the scene and I tease him, with an edge to my voice: 'Look! Such a pretty fish!'

That is the final take. The adventure has come to a close, the family is splitting up. The 'gypsies' pull down their tents and leave. Each of us takes a little something and goes our own way. The movie, the teamwork, the pieced-together family: all over. Cut!

Actors are used to break-ups. It's a staccato kind of profession, a disjointed life. You pack and repack, everything is on, then off – Go, stop! Go, stop! One has to be very strong.

I soon created a loyal little family to roam around this homeless world with me. Hairstylist, make-up artist, driver ... not indulgences but landmarks.

Goodbye, Emmanuelle. I gave you my flesh, brought you alive, made you come. Sylvia did her little turn, drew attention to herself. I existed, I was a centre of attention, I got what I wanted.

The film is finished, long live the film!

'Emmanuelle's body sings a love song, heart beating where it doesn't belong ...'* I love this music I am discovering for the first time. The singer-songwriter is Pierre Bachelet. Pierre is exactly how I'd imagined from this gentle, poetic song that still sometimes runs through my mind.

During the shooting of the film, producer Yves Rousset-Rouard introduces me to Jacques Itah; he and I hit it off immediately. He becomes my agent, and thanks to him I land a small part in Alain Robbe-Grillet's *Playing with Fire.* Robbe-Grillet is quite a character, erudite and with hair like a mad professor's. Hugo tells me that he's part of the 'nouveau roman' movement. Robbe-Grillet's other films include *L'Immortelle, Trans-Europ-Express* and *Successive Slidings of Pleasure.* My first scene in *Playing with Fire* is disturbing and sadomasochistic: my hands are bound, my skirt is torn and I have been whipped. I am reassured only by the kindness and skill of my fellow actors, Jean-Louis Trintignant and Philippe

* Translation (McLean) of the original, '*Mélodie d'amour chante le corps d'Emmanuelle qui bat coeur à corps perdu ...*'

Noiret! We become friends for the duration – I remember lovely warm dinners with Jean-Louis, Nadine, Philippe and his wife Monique.

Playing with Fire . . . that could be the title of my life story.

The news is bad. *Emmanuelle* will be restricted to the pornographic cinemas and not granted general release in France. The producer refuses to release the film in France under those condemning conditions. We wait. Censorship is a very formal process. The Culture Minister and the Censorship Panel have this to say: 'Inspired by the novel of the same name, the film endeavours to spread a message of cruel, voluptuous erotic questing which, as well as damaging contemporary values and morals, leads, apparently on purpose, to a questioning of normal human responses. For this reason the panel considers that it would in any case be subject to an X certificate. But two scenes bringing into question the respect due to the human body – the cigarette scene and an explicit sodomy sequence – seem to the panel to justify in this case a total ban . . .'

A few months after the death of Georges Pompidou, President Giscard d'Estaing's censors liked to think themselves more modern and tolerant. *Emmanuelle* was released on a normal French distribution circuit, with an X certificate, on 26 June 1974. The film was engulfed in scandal, which led to queues around the block. The cinemas couldn't get hold of enough copies – couriers rushed around frantically circulating them between screenings.

The producer called me and told me the news.

'It's a triumph, Sylvia! A triumph! You are a star!'

'I'm glad people want to watch our film.'

That was the kind of moderate, purely Calvinist reply I must have given him, faced with such euphoria. And yet the success was genuine, enormous.

Hugo took me to the Champs-Elysées.

'Come and see, it's worth it!'

We arrived by taxi. The cinema was called Le Triomphe, which made me smile. People were waiting patiently in a huge long queue, as they used to for rations. An excited and curious crowd who'd been deprived of exoticism, freedom, escape, sex.

Above them was an enormous billboard of Giacobetti's photo of me sitting in a rattan armchair.

The image looks timeless. In fact the chair is not Thai, not the one we used in the film, which was plaited rattan with a lovely dark patterned crown; the chair in the poster is much more ordinary, made in a Philippines factory and bought in Paris. But it still makes a perfect contrast to my European face, inviting the viewer far away, to lands where everything is possible. A throne as flimsy and temporary as desire.

'All these people have come just to see you. It's more than a success, it's a phenomenon.'

I huddle into the taxi seat, taking Hugo's hand and murmuring: 'It's wonderful, I'm very happy.'

This success arrives abruptly, like a wave breaking on a calm sea. It will sweep me away, I can feel it. I curl up small in the face of danger, sinking into the seat, turning my head away.

The Spanish are only just emerging from Franco's dictatorial rule, and flock to Perpignan in their thousands. It's the first time anyone has travelled so far just to see a film.

'But it's not a film they're going to see, it's a liberation!'

This migration over the border is the best possible publicity.

Senior officials from Muslim countries travel to France to watch in the embassies this film forbidden in their own lands. Travel agencies include it in their Paris itineraries: Sacré-Coeur, Moulin Rouge, *Emmanuelle* on the Champs-Elysées.

The press invades my life, journalists arrive from all over the world.

Hugo is assailed too.

'How does your partner's success affect you? Is it hard being the boyfriend of a sex symbol? What's it like being in her shadow? How does it feel that your work is less well known than *Emmanuelle*?'

'I am delighted about Sylvia's success.'

Hugo is intelligent, strong, and amused.

I will remain on my exotic throne on the Champs-Elysées for thirteen years. More than nine million French people will go to see me at the cinema. *Emmanuelle* will be a triumph in every European country, in America and in Japan.

50

How does a star live? Probably much as I did, from 1974 onwards. When you're a star you're never alone. You are surrounded. A small, obedient court takes shape around you:

- A driver-cum-bodyguard, my dear funny Marcel, who maintains a passionate relationship with the white Cadillac I treated myself to. I had wanted to swan around in my starmobile but the exotic and spotless conveyance spends its time smoking at the side of the road while I finish my shopping on foot, laughing, and Marcel grumbles and scolds his beautiful, capricious machine.
- A make-up artist who flatters me, and gives me a fresh complexion whatever time I went to bed.
- A hairdresser whose time is wasted on my boyish hairstyle.
- A press attaché who speaks several languages and behaves as if she were me.
- An industrious, discreet, methodical PA who does all my mundane tasks such as booking haircuts, paying bills and attending apartment-block meetings.
- A personal trainer who forces me to run when that's all I ever do.
- A photographer: only one, the one who knows my best profile, best light, best pose. Christian Simonpietri swapped

war photography for me, but I'm not sure it was any more restful!

A star's home is chic – a vast apartment in St-Germain-des-Prés. She wears sunglasses even at night and looks only far ahead. A star doesn't say much in public, she saves herself for the press and her movies, keeping people waiting. She speaks only in short sentences and her voice is always soft, murmuring – except occasionally, in a fit of pique. A star is soon exhausted because everything is moving too fast, and so she must rest. A star receives requests for advertising contracts that she refuses because she is a star, and invitations to inaugurate half of Paris, which she refuses too. I do agree excitedly to a life-size model of my measurements at Chanel, a female torso made out of cotton and inscribed with my name, 'Mlle Sylvia Kristel'; a motionless double, stored in the secret passages of that temple of sophistication, next to the other millionaire female torsos – stars and princesses. I always get the very best tables at restaurants and wherever I go I'm asked for autographs, which I love. I sign my name on all kinds of things – menus, the back of Métro season tickets, other people's photographs.

Enthusiasm comes spontaneously to life around me, a large entourage constantly smiling and wanting to please.

When you're a star, people are always saying 'of course!' and their speech is littered with 'darling!' It's true what they say – being a star means being loved. And how delightful that is, while it lasts.

My life as a true star lasted about ten years. It came to an end just as I was starting to believe in it.

*

No longer being a star is the opposite of all that I've just described, with the bonus of accumulated emotional debt, evident in the tendency to spiteful anger of those who previously revered you. At this stage one realises how unbearable that devotion and self-effacement must have been to them.

Sooner or later the debt must be paid. The beautiful pay more dearly than others – women are charged a great deal for having been beautiful, unfairly different, attractive; for provoking unsatisfied desire.

I recently watched a TV programme where the presenter was mocking an absent Catherine Deneuve, saying in front of a sniggering audience that it was 'time for granny to retire', and some other bitter person was also badmouthing this supremely talented, barely aged and still exceptionally beautiful actress.

Women force themselves to stay beautiful. It's a duty, an addiction, the ultimate generosity. Beautiful stars should be given some kind of immunity, so they can age in peace until they pass away in the soft light of their memories, protected from the hatred of those bent on revenge, from the screens that present them as continually young and sprightly, and from the disappointment of a frank public still subject to the charm of the elderly woman's films, and who shriek loudly in the street: 'Bloody hell, she's looking old!'

We should shield women from this pain, thanking them instead for the dream they have provided – at such a price – of a life made softer and more beautiful, awaiting nothing in return except love, immense love. That's what a star is: a love addict.

51

'I'd like to have your baby. Let's make a family.'

Hugo is surprised, and smiles.

'OK, if you think that's a good idea.'

Yes, it was a good idea, an obvious and necessary step, a link to the reality I was allowing to slip out of my grasp. I was young and fertile.

One morning I wake up with a new certainty: I am pregnant. An inexplicable feeling, an intuition, the physical sensation that the inside of my body has changed profoundly in the space of one night. Hugo is already up, reading in the living room.

'I think I'm pregnant. In fact I'm sure of it. Did you make love to me last night?'

Hugo feigns surprise then smiles.

I sleep well next to Hugo. He makes me feel safe. I know his body. When night comes the exhaustion of this unreal life – this constant act – covers me with a soft, heavy fog. My body loses its rigidity, my bearing relaxes, I melt into the warmth of the man who looks after me and wants only the best for me. I fall asleep. My sleep is sometimes so deep that I have no memory of the night at all, not the slightest disturbance, or noise, or startling, just the beginning of the night and its fog. Hugo is a nocturnal being. He comes and goes, full of life, free and alone; he writes, he desires me. At night I sleep, find respite. Not him.

I confide my morning intuition – certitude – to my friend Monique; she laughs. A few weeks later the doctor will confirm that I am indeed pregnant. I remember smiling in the taxi, and the touch of Monique, who has come with me. The air is soft, we don't talk, I am thinking about what is happening inside me, delighted with this mysterious reproduction, this magical reward, this new starring role.

Arthur was born on 10 February 1975 in Amsterdam. I loved my son from the very first moment, with a surprising, unsettling love. An unshakeable bond was born. The existence of my son began the maturing of the child I had been. I had made something, a true reflection of myself; I was becoming gradually, deeply self-sufficient, and more and more perturbed by this new being. My life changed slowly and irreversibly. I stopped dreaming. I became a mother, less loving, less young, less ethereal as Hugo said, but a mother, holding in her arms a part of herself, separate, calm, restless, disruptive. Arthur didn't leave my side. He never would leave me, he couldn't – we were bonded for life.

52

I extended my intimate, protective, motivating entourage to include Marcel's uncle Jacques Itah (my exuberant *pied-noir* manager), and Monique Kouznetzoff as my communications adviser. Monique was more than an adviser, she was a loyal friend – a rare thing in that fickle world. I loved her style, her strength, her discipline, her sense of nuance, her plunging necklines and her keen business sense. Monique knew everyone, and everyone loved Monique. We didn't see each other for almost thirty years but then took up again where we'd left off, full of nostalgia and the delightful desire to make up for lost time.

My new and real families mix well. Hugo, Arthur and Marianne come everywhere with me. Marianne and Marcel squabble in the most delightful way. My baby sister is becoming somebody, taking up more space, moulding herself. Her voice has changed, her accent is more refined. Marcel teases her constantly, repeating her orders in the exact same high-pitched voice, which drives Marianne mad and makes me howl with laughter. My mother is often around too, watching over her little flock. My extended family cossets and warms me, providing the human continuity I need to deal with the extremity of the encounters, feelings and settings of my new profession.

Even patient Hugo eventually gets fed up with tripping over international TV cables first thing in the morning; they practically live with us in St-Germain. I have failings, the biggest perhaps being my inability to say no. 'No' is an abrupt, contemptuous, flat word which cuts through things and is foreign to me. So it's yes to everything – interviews in magazines of every shape and form, on radio, television . . . yes to attention in every shape, to this wonderful influx, this sense of being at the centre, the heart, being of interest. Bulimia fed by the fear that the attention will stop.

I particularly like newspaper interviews. You have to pose for photos, and express yourself. I get off on the surprise of journalists who expect me to be a bimbo. My mother is still cutting everything out, tracking me in the magazines.

'You've got to go to the dentist!' Monique insists.

'Is that the most exciting thing you can come up with?'

'To deal with your baby tooth, Sylvia! It's too visible in profile shots. You can't promote sexual liberation and be an erotic icon, yet keep your baby teeth!'

I loved my baby tooth. I could feel it under my tongue, fragile, worn, little, slightly wobbly but tenacious.

I did go to the dentist. He smiled as he pulled it out, practically with his bare hands. He showed it to me; it had no roots.

'Do you want to keep it?'

'No . . .'

He placed it carefully in a little tin box and closed the lid. I think he kept it.

53

They organise a promotional world tour of *Emmanuelle*. The producer asks me to be in two further films. I accept. A contract is tangible proof of success, a rational, serious, durable thing in this airy world no more solid than a helium balloon.

Two more films, meaning the adventure will have a sequel – likewise adapted from an Emmanuelle Arsan novel, *The Anti-Virgin* – and a third part whose name has not yet been decided.

'*Goodbye Emmanuelle!*' I suggest, wanting to bring the story to an end; one day I'll have to do something new.

London. Formal presentation to the Queen Mother. It seems we have a lot in common – apparently she's mischievous, curious and drinks spirits on a daily basis.

I am flattered. Jaeckin comes with me. We are organised into rows as at boarding school, with me in the front row and Jaeckin behind. The Queen Mother walks down the line, followed at the correct distance by her daughter Margaret. Her smile is shrewd but kind. She advances, pausing regularly to hold out her spotless gloved hand. A train of the well-dressed and completely fascinated masses (of which I am part) follows in her wake. Her Majesty is coming closer and I go over my most graceful curtsy in my head. My heart is beating fast. Is she going to walk smilingly, royally past, not seeing me? Or will she do me the honour of a snippet of conversation, ennobling me with her quiet, neutral words? Does she really know who I am? I am told she is perfectly informed and there are no accidents in this etiquette, this gathering of celebrities.

The lady with the pink hat, pink bag and pink shoes, the single-hued lady, impeccably and simply visible, is coming towards me. My back becomes ramrod-straight, my chin lifts, I attempt a slight smile; I want to be like her, worthy of her, to blend in. The flashes intensify, emanating blinding white light, the diamonds are sparkling, the crown is real. I blink and see a hand held out, white, poised, perfectly straight. I grasp it with the tips of my fingers, barely listening, bowing and nodding in slow motion. I murmur: 'Thank you ... thank you for this honour.' Jaeckin suddenly elbows in. He wants to be in the photo. He jostles me a little, introduces himself, bows. Her Highness is unshakeable, motionless; her powdered skin is like porous marble, nothing can divert the movement of her eyes. She gently takes back the hand she has lent me and waits a moment while I raise the head I barely dare show; just long enough to look at me with shining, benevolent intention. The Queen Mother goes on her way.

54

'You don't know Tokyo? You'll love it! You'll have a fantastic time. Shopping, raw fish, neon everywhere and people smiling all the time ... it's wonderful! Don't be paranoid, they're not making fun of you, they're welcoming you – you'll see, it's bizarre. In any case you won't understand a word, which is for the best. The names of the streets, the people, the food in restaurants will all be Chinese to you! Well, Japanese.'

My manager Jacques makes me laugh.

Japan is a unique, unimaginable country, a totally different world. Nothing is the same, or familiar; it is truly foreign. The welcome they subjected me to remains for me a supreme example of the capacity for excess of this strange nation, at the opposite extreme from the Calvinist moderation of my countrymen. The Japanese culture may be obedient but the people, once enflamed, can create a most extraordinary mass movement. Their identikit, constrained nature can explode on account of a different possibility, a symbol of freedom. They adopted and celebrated me ardently. The women applauded my character's erotic charisma and her power over the man; a passive power, control of the man by his own desire, making him believe that he is leading the dance when in fact he is following.

For the Japanese women this power was symbolised by the love scene in which I turn my husband over onto his back and sit astride him, imposing the rhythm of my body. This scene really affected them; it made me into a living monument to freedom.

The flashes blind me. I hide my face because the flight was so long that I'm afraid of looking ugly. The crowd of journalists that surges up to me as I get out of the plane is polite and extremely large. The same mob at the entrance to the hotel – everywhere this great fervour. I am flattered, delighted and groggy. Imagine the effect of this powerful testimony, this dazzling proof you've dreamed of and are now finding just where you weren't expecting it, provided by unknown men and women utterly different from yourself. The inhabitants of another world giving you abundantly that which you lack the most, with such naive, childlike enthusiasm. The Japanese resemble their bonsai, those miniature trees I discover with awe, pruned every day to stop them growing. This pint-sized, innocent, good nation gave me its enormous affection. Japan is one of my favourite memories.

After the emotion of the welcome, I remember the enthusiastic advice of my agent: 'Shopping!' Now there's a word that lives in me like a prayer, a command I am always delighted to carry out.

'You can't have thought it through!'

My local press attaché is in shock.

'Of course I have.'

'But, Sylvia, you don't seem to understand. These people are here for you, they've gathered at the hotel door, lying in wait for you. They will follow you, monopolise you, want to touch you, cut off a lock of your hair; it's traditional! They will trample you and we'll find you scalped, in several pieces!'

'Really? But I'd love to go shopping ...' I am quite insistent.

'Very well, Sylvia. Give me the names of the shops you'd like to visit and I will take care of everything.'

I give the names of the designers I like, adding 'plus local flavour'.

I do my shopping in boutiques closed to the public, sad and silent shops with sweet, helpful salesgirls. I am experiencing the new and strange sensation of having to protect myself from too great a fervour, of no longer being in control of the effect I produce.

I decide to buy myself a fur coat, a fitting accessory for a star. I hesitate between a heavy mink and a more close-fitting raincoat with a splendid silver-fox stole, a bastion of softness against the world. I try them on one after the other, unable to decide.

'What is this lovely fur lining?' I ask the salesgirl.

The raincoat is lined with a fine, silky, warm, dark brown fur.

'It's a rare fur, Canadian squirrel.'

'Squirrel?!'

I think immediately of the school coat rack, of that sneering squirrel forced upon me. I stroke the fur, sad and rather satisfied. I am remembering. Was that yesterday, or another life? It was before, and yet it's all still here, a hair's breadth away. My childhood is right here under my fingers.

'I'll take this one!'

'Which?'

'The squirrel.'

I've been invited onto the red carpet at Cannes, and Hugo has come with me. The room at the Carlton is glorious and this morning we went out sailing with some influential producers. My dress has been delivered. It's gorgeous – a shimmering, backless silk. The weather is mild, the sun shining. I walk out onto the balcony. A dense crowd is moving towards La Croisette – a gang of happy, brightly dressed onlookers, the same that in a few hours will gather at the foot of the steps to watch the stars pass. My attention is drawn to a laugh, louder than the rest. A tipsy tourist at the foot of the Palais is pointing out the hotel windows, then me, and saying to the kid at his side: 'Look, that's the Carlton. That's where they sleep, the stars, up there, where we'll never go!'

I immediately retreat back into the room, concealing myself behind the curtains. In a few hours a limousine will come for us; I will walk out of the main hotel entrance, not wearing shades because at Cannes one is there to be seen. Then, when I step out of the elongated car in my party dress and diamonds, flashing a delighted smile and stretching out my hand to wave at the crowd which may perhaps recognise me, celebrate me, when I give myself, light-heartedly, to the pleasure of being welcomed in style to this temple of film, when I give myself happily to the public – the only star-maker – just then I may hear the Carlton tourist, a little drunker and more bitter now, yelling from the bottom of the steps: 'Look, there's the slut from *Emmanuelle*!'

No one has ever called me that, and yet I never stop worrying about it. It's my way of expressing the part of me that rejects this role, this image of me. A daughterly, inherited part, a religious voice which would stand fiercely against that which I am becoming almost in spite of myself: a sexual object, a reduced, symbolic woman. Beneath all the glitter, the smiles, the cameras, the sun shining as it is today, I am sometimes tortured by the embarrassment and fear of being punished, banished, as in that Thai police station. Perhaps I *have* committed an irreparable sin, shown what should be forever hidden, accepted that which one should refuse. Have I betrayed my own self, and those who made me?

The car drives slowly up to the foot of the steps. There had been quite a stir as we left the hotel. Every television channel in the world is posted along the red staircase. The eyes of the world are upon us, my mother of course will be watching too, everyone . . . I share my fears with Hugo.

'What if they insult me?'

'Of course they won't! Relax, this is Cannes – scandal is far too common, and this crowd are film lovers, they're nice. Smile, be generous, pause, sign autographs. Give them back a little of what they give you, and everything will be fine.'

I am afraid. I'm tempted to tell the driver to take us back to the hotel. Hugo feels my anxiety; the silence is oppressive, and he takes my hand.

'You're so silly, my darling . . .'

The car door opens smoothly, I get out as gracefully as possible. All of a sudden I can't bear my naked back, it's totally obscene, a provocation too far. I smile, trembling.

'Sylvia! Sylvia! Emmanuelle!'

I turn round each time someone calls my name, trying to smile at everyone. I want them to understand who I am, to know me at last, to carry on calling my name, loving me, letting me believe and dream. I need this.

I sign autographs, kiss a few people, squeeze a few hands that won't let go, wave with my arm outstretched, blow kisses, turn round again and again, giving myself with delight.

Hugo takes my arm and we climb the steps, one by one, rising, moving away. The cameras flash, the photographers are calling me, some shouting: 'By yourself! By yourself!' I pose for a few seconds then we carry on, moving forward in an electric, joyful clamour. I was afraid for nothing. I won't be publicly humiliated. Before stepping inside the Palais there's a final landing, perfect for a last gesture to the public. With the greatest of pleasure, I give a big wave to this friendly crowd; the air is warm, the breeze light and the silk of my dress laps softly against my thighs.

'Aren't you ashamed, screwing around stark naked?!'

The words are bellowed from my right. I don't look, I remain frozen, smiling, the entrance is just behind me, I can feel a draught of cool air from that direction. The uniformed guard adorning the steps motions me to enter with a troubled smile. Hugo squeezes my hand and kisses my neck. A few flashes are still going off. We walk in.

That was the one and only time I heard that sort of comment, but it was enough to nurture a lifetime's fear of insult. I cannot wait alone on a pavement, or meet people at street corners. I get consumed by panic that someone will pause, notice that this idle and still beautiful woman is alone, recognise and then insult me.

I will always be afraid of insult – to me, my mother, the women I love, the women who made me.

Emmanuelle is by far the most successful French movie of 1974. I am feted for my screen presence, my power to evoke, my arousing essence, my unusualness, my role in the film's success. I am an image more than an actress, a compelling, extraterrestrial body. I intrigue the French world of film like some kind of rare species. I represent a new opportunity, and receive some lovely offers, fits of enthusiasm that do credit to me and that I accept like requests for my hand. The suitors are certainly high class: after Robbe-Grillet come Mocky, Chabrol, Vadim ... *Emmanuelle* was a fling – now I'll get engaged, and then married.

No Pockets in a Shroud is a detective film by Jean-Pierre Mocky. I hadn't known the word 'shroud', meaning the dress of the dead. *No Pockets in a Shroud*: just like my uniform at the restaurant. The title may be obscure but Jean-Pierre Mocky is a great film-maker. He was always gentle and patient with me. Less so with my male colleagues – perhaps I charmed him. Jean-Pierre liked women, and he also liked my voice: 'Such velvet!' He used my voice, a first for me in a French film. Michael Lonsdale and Jean-Pierre Marielle are the same in real life as on screen. Michael taciturn, focused, disturbing but kind. I played his wife, whom he tries to kill with a gun. He was so permeated by his role and therefore by hatred that I was scared for real, and even asked them to check his gun! Jean-Pierre Marielle is hugely talented as well as funny, spontaneous and straightforward. I remember a scene where we had to dance together. Jean-Pierre didn't like dancing, for him it was a kind of stunt, something he was forced to do and would much rather have not. I found the stiffness of his body, his lack of coordination and his overt discomfort irresistible. We laughed a lot. As he tried to spin me round he called out: 'Lead the dance, lass. I'll follow – for now!'

I respect the contract that binds me to producer Yves Rousset-Rouard and, as if burying my adolescence, shoot the sequel to Emmanuelle's adventures, known in English by the title *Emmanuelle: The Joys of a Woman*. I will continue to work, to act, as agreed. *Emmanuelle*'s triumph has given me a taste for success and ease. I will redo the same thing, in a different setting. I will give once more what I have already given. Like a kiss, reminiscent of the first but still pleasant, infinitely repeatable.

Hong Kong? Why not – for Emmanuelle Arsan the exotic is always Asiatic. Hugo accompanies me for the last time. Arthur stays in Holland.

The director, Francis Giacobetti, is the person who took the *Emmanuelle* poster photograph. He is known for his soft-core erotic photography. Francis is brilliant at capturing a moment; he is master of the image but not of movement. Actors move on their own, they can even be hard to control, and the scope of the task is too much for Francis. He often bursts helplessly into tears. The film has a big budget, and the Japanese financiers are in a hurry. The story matters less than the release date – *Joys of a Woman* has already been pre-sold worldwide. The film's first scene is written on the aeroplane that takes Hugo and me to Hong Kong. The script is written from one day to the next, and because of this wait the crew has plenty of time to polish the lighting and put finishing touches to the set. It will be visually magnificent.

In Asia I catch a virus: a rare, badly treated eye infection bleaches out my iris and forces me to shoot several scenes in sunglasses, but more importantly will leave me partially blind in my left eye for the rest of my life.

We finish filming *Joys of a Woman* in December 1975. The film is released almost everywhere in the world except France, where it is censored and given an X certificate despite containing no pornography whatsoever. It's the turn of my French fans to travel to see me in Belgium or Spain. Times are changing.

The producer institutes proceedings against the French government, which is perhaps dreading a fresh surge of harmful erotica. Yves Rousset-Rouard will win the case two years later; the film will be released, but with the proviso that its subversive French title (*The Anti-Virgin*) be replaced.

Emmanuelle 2 is a success rather than a triumph – the second kiss pleased less than the first.

Jacques Itah gives me the script for Vadim's *A Faithful Woman*. The adjective suits me well, I am faithful. Isn't that the true nature of woman? I don't spread myself thin, I am monogamous.

Vadim really sees me. He enjoys casting against type and imagines me exactly opposite to my licentious image, wanting to reveal another side of me to the public. Sylvia Kristel as seen by Vadim – as he's done with others.

On the set of *A Faithful Woman* I become friends with the lively, delightful and extremely beautiful Nathalie Delon.

I ask her curiously about her famous ex-husband, whom I find fascinating.

'So, what's he like? Come on, tell me!'

Nathalie smiles at this question she's been asked a hundred times, and doesn't reply. She stands up, creates a diversion, hums a tune, changes the subject and by her silence adds fuel to my fascination. I was waiting for a revelation, a secret confided woman-to-woman, a clue to clarify the mystery or at least get a little closer to it. Nothing. Nathalie won't say anything, she'll do a few impressions but that's all; understandably she's tired of still existing primarily through a marriage.

I'm not dealing well with my boredom, or the interminable waiting forced upon actors. When I'm not shooting I go and watch the others. I am alone and restless. Hugo has only visited the set once, briefly. He left quickly, complaining of the cold. Hugo is distancing himself, tired of living with my entourage; he needs his space and is weary of the world of film. He wants to return to his poetry and I let him – I am adrift too. That's just how it is.

Vadim is very attentive, with a gentle charm; he is funny despite himself, he likes to party, he asks me out and I accept, following his lead.

I let myself be seduced and, unable to share myself, tell Hugo about this crush. We decide to take a break.

Vadim isn't really handsome but he's tall and affectionate and I need his warmth. Watching him unfurl out of his Fiat 500 and smooth down his bohemian clothes is an irresistible sight. He is fickle, mischievous, apparently shy. He arouses compassion with his wide-eyed, slightly sad smile; maternal fervour for this Slavic child whose charm is his greatest talent.

Women love Vadim, they cluster around him, all beautiful whether they're ex-girlfriends or future conquests. His fickleness creates an invigorating lack of security; nothing will ever be permanent with this changeable man.

I will pass the time with him, most pleasantly. I will come on-set excited about a nascent bond whose outcome I cannot tell. I mind less about the future than the pleasure of the moment. Vadim is a pleasure person.

Unusually, our liaison continues after the film. Love affairs normally last only as long as the shoot, like those holiday romances that happen spontaneously and for a set period of time. The 'extended family' of the film, formed for the duration, isn't enough to overcome the loneliness and boredom of the actor, and love affairs are inevitable, a driving force.

Vadim never has any money. I'm not sure if he spends it all or doesn't earn any. He's a penniless celebrity, a not uncommon type. Vadim is a passionate gambler. It's more than a hobby, it's a way of life. He is swarming with ideas. He wants us to invest in a horse-racing company, a woolly-minded plan that my Dutch thriftiness protects me from.

I am headhunted by a Japanese company to be the face of a coffee brand. I usually refuse this kind of proposal, but this time the scale of the fee merits consideration. I accept, on condition that Vadim, the stony-broke genius, directs the promotional film. The Japanese cede to my demands. These are my years of distorting fame – people rarely say no, and the entire world seems to agree with me. The usual giddiness of success.

Vadim asks that we film in St-Tropez because spring is always wonderful there.

'You'll see, at this time of year the colours are exceptionally intense, unbelievably luminous!'

It is bucketing down in St-Tropez, which I am visiting for the first time. The sky is so low one can almost touch it, thick, solid, dark grey. It pours down apocalyptically, horrifying the Japanese crew. The unexpectedly awful weather and the histrionic distress of the Japanese provoke in both me and the purveyor of sunny blue skies a sense of humour that will last the entire shoot. We spend our time in cafés waiting for the sun to reappear. We drink heavily to feed our laughter, our carefree feelings, our infinitely pleasant love affairs. We wait in vain; this unseasonable monsoon is tenacious. The Japanese suggest renting a yacht and shooting in the cabin. The entire crew is made to shake the boat in dock to give the impression of being out at sea. A spotlight is placed outside the porthole to evoke the St-Tropez sun, and my clothes are flimsy despite the cold. I've absolutely no desire to sip coffee at each and every take, so my cup will contain brown rum instead. A smoke-machine is hired to simulate the warmth of steaming fresh coffee with his exhalations. I keep bursting out laughing. The Japanese aren't best pleased. Tough – it is a happy time in my life.

Vadim used to talk film with me, telling me all about that complex world whose codes he understood. He loved history, the origins of countries and peoples, and art. He contributed to my apprenticeship.

Vadim was *joie de vivre* laid over pain – lyrical, sensitive and tinged with nostalgia. He was always brimful of ideas, projects that for the most part would come to nothing. I would like to express my tenderness for this nomadic man, this whimsical sensualist, this warm wind caressing you as he passed.

Our affair could not withstand the torrential rains of St-Tropez. We left each other with no mention of a split, simply saying goodbye. Off he went, and I returned home to Paris, to Hugo.

My absence doesn't seem to have affected him. Hugo has rediscovered his friends and his world of the noble arts, and is splitting his time between France and his native Belgium. He is focused inwards, on his creativity, his self-expression. My son accompanies me almost everywhere, all the time, wherever I travel or film. I employ someone to look after him when I am unavailable and my mother and sister often come with me to help.

My child is a bastion, an anchor, he helps keep my life in balance.

Hugo will show an interest in Arthur later, when he can speak, lay claim to himself, exist as an independent, thinking being. Hugo is not moved by early childhood. Quite the contrary – that time of life conjures up nothing sweet for him at all. Life is worth something only in its distinction, its autonomy and individual added value. Hugo doesn't care for that dependent time during which the fragile human shapes himself.

My love for my son is instinctive, immediate, far from intellectual. Maternal instinct or simply a great desire to love, to give myself without thought?

*

Fading love is a sorry sight. I had thought my love for Hugo immortal – I've doubted God sometimes, but never love. And yet I can feel myself falling out of love. My withdrawal symptoms are decreasing, my heartbeat remains steady, the other that I used to love no longer wields that intense influence, no longer seems to emit the radiance that lit up my life and gave it sense. Love is fading, slowly and surely. It's a human love, which lives, weakens and then comes to an end. It has a life cycle, a term. So this is the end I had thought impossible, the gentle decline.

My split with Hugo is not yet spoken. We keep going, trying to stay together; we have a child, we strive for a new balance, a less intense life together. We struggle on.

I become Alice in Chabrol's film *Alice or the Final Fleeing*.

Alice reminds me of Emmanuelle in Wonderland, which is how I felt at the beginning of the shoot, when we first arrived in Thailand. In order to lighten the load of my role, to retain my innocence and prolong belief in the dream, I'd decided to tell journalists that *Emmanuelle* was a kind of *Alice in Wonderland*.

It is Alice's death that Claude Chabrol offers me. A strange, surreal tale, an exploration of the journey into death, of the mysterious moment that precedes it. So once more I am an inspiration for death: Mocky, Chabrol ... perhaps desire and death are related? Is desire so unbearable that we wish to see it dead?

Claude is funny, greedy, attentive, filthy and shrewd. He appreciates refinement as much as coarseness. My French is still not perfect. I hear him shouting '*Bonne bourre!*' after each sentence, instead of goodbye.

'*Bonne bourre*'? I've no idea what this means.

'What does "*bonne bourre*" mean?' I ask Claude.

He laughs out loud and seizes this irresistible opportunity to make the shoot even more lively.

'It's a casual, affectionate expression that means ... good-bye!'

That's new. It must be one of those regional expressions I'm discovering in particular parts of France.

As everyone is going home tired at the end of the day, I kiss my actor, technician and support colleagues goodbye, boldly uttering the new phrase, proud of my slang. Instead of saying 'See you tomorrow', I enthusiastically shout '*Bonne bourre!*' Some laugh, others just look shocked. A handsome technician replies, 'With pleasure!', but my make-up artist, a respectable mother and wife, is horrified. No one dares tell me the real meaning of the words. Emmanuelle shouts '*Bonne bourre!*' each evening to a hilarious crew which understands, from Chabrol's tears of laughter, the source of this new leitmotif. Emmanuelle saying '*Bonne bourre!*' rather than 'goodbye' is very fitting – at least I'm living up to my image.

However, my make-up artist becomes more and more hostile to my unwitting familiarity, and one evening opens her heart.

'What on earth are you doing, speaking like that?'

'I'm sorry?'

I laughed hard before abandoning the expression, which had become common parlance on-set – except when saying goodbye to Claude, depraved sweetie that he is, especially when his wife was around.

Charles Vanel, Jean-Louis Trintignant, André Dussollier,

Jean Carmet, Michel Galabru, Michael Lonsdale, Jean-Pierre Marielle, Gérard Depardieu, Michel Piccoli ... the list of my work colleagues from that time is impressive. Here's to you, artists! I met subtle, complex, gifted, multifaceted people who enchanted me. I had the good fortune of rubbing shoulders with real talent. I learned my craft from them, on-set, observing humbly and minutely.

Walerian Borowczyk, director of *Immoral Tales*, offers me the lead role in *The Margin*, adapted from the Goncourt-winning novel by André Pieyre de Mandiargues. It is a strong role, perhaps my favourite. Walerian seemed haunted by his erotic fantasies, by his taste for fetishism. I play a prostitute.

I have never sold my sexuality, just mimed that of another. Although actually my body does have a price – my fee is printed in black and white in all my contracts. My body has a fluctuating market value.

Hugo congratulates me heartily on my new role, I have surprised him. I am pleased with this acknowledgement. The film is not a success, and distribution is limited to the prettily named 'experimental, art-house circuit'. Few people saw me in it, which is a shame.

Hugo doesn't come on-set any more, and my loneliness and boredom are increasing. You have to either forget your solitude or put an end to it. My love of champagne grows until it's a contractual requirement. That was my idea – it's rather glamorous and means I no longer have to ask. Sylvia Kristel drinks Dom Perignon on contract. The quantity is specified; an excessive amount that I claim to share. On certain days the gentleness of champagne doesn't seem to hit the mark, so I ask for cognac. In my bag I carry some extremely strong herbal mints. Little bombs that I suck quickly, making me contort my mouth like a rodent before a take. The concentrated mint ploughs through my nose and throat, creating great clean alleyways through which the air surges, intense and sharp, going to my head and firing me up. 'Action!'

Film shoots become my sites of mild debauchery. I am still young and lucid, but out of my depth. I am very quick to start paying back the price of success, of scandal, of standing out. I pay in kind with my own currency. I give my body, and destroy it. On film sets with nothing to do, I drink, forget and laugh. I begin a new dance, a new rite, a carousel of lovers: an assistant director, a producer, a star ... it's easy for an actor to seduce, charm is a widespread commodity in the movies. The 1970s were a wonderful enclave between censorship and Aids. The sexual liberation was real.

I realise my powers of attraction and do not tire of exercising and confirming them. My seductions prove my influence, my importance. I get a real buzz from living out my desires straightforwardly, transgressing the rules of good conduct, playing.

On the set of Francis Girod's *René la Canne*, the great devourer Gérard Depardieu seeks out my favours. It's a funny sight. I feed myself on this gratifying feeling: being desirable and tasting desire, living it so as to believe in it.

Michel Piccoli is also in on the game, and Francis has a hard time taming these two headstrong men. Joyful improvisation takes over from the screenplay and I am the only one to respect the script, studious and intimidated.

Michel is a passionate, excessive, surprising man. He asks me out to dinner. I call at his hotel room and he comes to the door bare-chested, asking for another few minutes to get ready – among actors, getting dolled up is not only for the women. I am immediately struck by the thick, dark fur covering his body! He looks at me silently, then grabs a lighter and sets fire to the hair, right in front of me, not even flinching. A steak-house smell fills the room and he runs off to the bathroom laughing.

Gérard and Michel are extraordinary actors, limitless.

None of these 'normal' films was a success. I was disappointed and a little hurt. I was dressed, but people preferred me naked. I spoke, but they liked me better silent, or dubbed. I realised that the public had been deeply affected by *Emmanuelle* and wanted to prolong their fantasy, to keep me within it, symbolic and naked, idealised and necessary.

Roland Topor is a friend of Hugo's, a wonderful, multitalented artist. He dabbles in every form. He paints, sculpts and writes – poems, a column for *Hara Kiri* magazine, screenplays for Polanski ... he's a free man, outrageous, unspecialised. His expression is complete and uncompromising. He did that landmark Amnesty International-commissioned drawing of a man in profile, a handsome man, with large, simply drawn, almond-shaped eyes; his head has pivoted on a vertical neck and toppled backwards into an impossible right-angled position. The throat is vulnerable, offered up. A heavy hammer weighs on the man's outstretched chin, pushing the head down and back as if it's a piece of wood. The man is being deprived of speech by violent physical oppression. The power of the image comes from its softness. The hammer is breaking the man's jaw but his features remain mild. He is almost smiling, his opposition pacifist, his enthusiasm tenacious. His expression has been mutilated but will be reborn.

Topor's laugh echoes endlessly inside me. He died almost ten years ago but I still hear it. It was more than a laugh, it was a shout, an expression as powerful as his words, as his art.

'I would like to paint!' I tell him confidently.

Topor laughs, he was always laughing. He's not sneering, he's reacting. He tells me that I'm right, I must express myself authentically, must liberate myself. He invites me to lunch at his apartment-studio overlooking Paris. He has cooked, and the wine is plentiful and delicious.

'How does one paint?'

Topor laughs. He pours his wine into the food left on his plate, mixes it together and plunges his hands into the goo.

'With anything, everything! Be free! You have to follow through to the end. Further. Change the meaning of things, shock, live!'

I am hesitant to start. I sense that if I start painting, devoting myself to this art, I may lose interest in all other forms of expression. Hugo encourages me, fatherly and motivating. I owe him that liberation. I start painting in Paris, under his influence, bathed in his artistic milieu. I create unashamed naked bodies submitted to constraint, women, graceful or bizarre, all different. I want to marry beauty, femininity and excess, provocation and sometimes violence.

I can remember my first work of art. It was already pro-vocative but gentle, a mixture of petals and blood. That was a long time ago. I laid my nascent talent before the eyes of my indifferent, conventional mother. It was at the hotel. I was a kid and there was blood on the lounge lampshade. A peasant had put a small glass in his pocket and the waiter had seen him and asked for the stolen object. The peasant had denied it, become angry and slashed the waiter's hand with his curved knife. The blood had spurted, Aunt Mary had shouted and threatened to call the police. My mother had come down, everyone had left. All that remained were the stains.

My mother, upset, grumbled about this waste that no one would pay for. Then she thought a moment and said to me: 'Sylvia, get some paints and draw on this, coloured shapes like at school, it'll keep you busy.'

I complied. I left the violent red of the blood as the heart of tulip petals, outlining it with compensatory pastels. The sizes varied according to the extent of the stains. I was proud of my efforts. Aunt Alice congratulated me.

'You left the blood visible?' said my mother.

'Yes, the red was pretty. Do you like it?'

My mother stared wide-eyed. She had wanted to conceal, I knew that. But I had displayed, embellished. She looked, intrigued, at my blood-red flowers. They weren't childlike flowers. The lines were sharp and graceful. My mother saw my talent, my life-like, engaging and violent drawing, and said: 'Go to your room, right now!'

That was my first work of art – blood tulips.

55

My agent Jacques Itah has negotiated me a contract for a large-scale Austro-American co-production, Ken Annakin's *The Fifth Musketeer*, adapted from the Alexandre Dumas novel. It's an important turning point in my career, the recognition of my value on the international market; I am 'bankable', a film can be made on my name. The resources are huge, the crew is made up of more than three hundred people from all around the world. The organisation is flawless, nothing is improvised, my hairdresser Madeleine comes with me as stated in my contract, the costumes are lavish, the cast impressive: Beau Bridges, Rex Harrison, Ursula Andress, Olivia de Havilland ... Versailles is reconstructed in an Austrian chateau. The winter is bitterly cold. I am the Spanish Infanta, so at least my skirts are thick.

I organise a little party in honour of Miss de Havilland. She is very touched, and dances all night long. Before slipping gracefully away she comes over to thank me.

'Thank you, dear Sylvia, for your thoughtfulness and care. Thank you so much, too, for this role ...'

Feeling shy, I look down and shake my head slightly.

'No, thank you, I feel privileged that you're here ... I didn't decide the cast, you know.'

'I know, but without your name, this film wouldn't have been made.'

I am intrigued by a handsome actor who always sits in a corner not speaking to anyone and reading the *Sunday Times* with total, irritating indifference. The Infanta goes up to him and raises her heavy skirts to reveal a worn pair of jeans; she points out a silver hip flask wedged into her cowboy boots. The man is amused and smiles, at last. I grab my flask and my first words are: 'Fancy a taste?'

My carousel of lovers will stop here, on this first big international shoot with this magnificent man, Ian McShane. He accepts my brandy, and I become intoxicated, ablaze. As does he.

Love at first sight is not luck, it's dangerous. Its roots are not in conscious reality. It's an immediate recognition, a direct meeting of two unconscious minds, a mysterious bridge. I have never probed my unconscious, that omnipresent force that directs my body, imprinting it with these incomprehensible, sometimes life-denying urges. I've seen my desirous, greedy, unreasonably attached body do the exact opposite of what would have been good for me. I've seen my compelling attraction to people who wanted to do me harm, who were avoiding their own destruction by provoking mine. I've seen my decline, my flight, a slow, gradual, unconscious debasement.

I would very much like to meet my unconscious. I imagine it as a kind of savage beast with scarred, scuffed fur, who lives in the dark, grunting and roaring, a lawless being with no respect or liking for me, waiting and primitive. I have left Freudian analysis to my neurotic girlfriends, never confronting the beast. I've even poked fun at dubious psychoanalytical practices. It all seemed hare-brained, hypothetical and expensive. A fad for intrinsically complicated stars. I did my analysis alone. I put a great deal of effort into it, understood more or less, forgave and forgave myself. It took me a lifetime, took my life, almost.

Ian is thirty-five years old. His body is like a fruit. He is that exact age where the beauty of youth is in its final flowering – exquisite, more stunning than ever for its finale, before the onset of the ageing process.

A fine, straight Grecian nose, big, pale, shining eyes, and dark eyebrows which are long and bushy but thinner at the edges, virile yet delicate, the sign of an exotic heritage. His smile is not a smile but a trap, a constant lifting of the curtain over wolf-like teeth, white fangs that really do bite. I am the perfect prey – he recognised me as such, and I knew he was a predator. I like being bitten into; this is all I could wish for. My attraction knows no bounds, the trap calls to me, the devil is irresistible. I will give him power of attorney to continue the task I have started alone and which sometimes costs me dear – my destruction, the conclusion of my ruin.

I leave Hugo. I tell him that I'm leaving. He is not terribly affected, he is familiar with break-ups, lives through them and uses them as material. Our union was bound to be temporary, we were too different . . . one has to try to explain. A few words from behind my sunglasses – I'm still a little shy with this great man, a little ashamed as well, sad about the mistake I can feel myself making, my bold choice, both wretched and irresistible. I am dependent on another, and leaving to be with him, to live out this addiction. A few small words to the father of my child, giving shape to something that happened a long time ago. Hugo takes my hand, he is not bitter, he wants this to end affectionately. I pull away, impatient. Hugo is no longer for me, he's too old, too well behaved, too static, too good. I don't deserve such benevolence.

Arthur? He stays with me. That's not debatable. We agree about that, it's obvious. I wanted my son, I will keep him. Hugo is supportive, accepting. Arthur is four years old, and follows me silently.

'Have you been drinking?'

Hugo takes my hand again.

'No . . .'

'You're lying.'

'No . . .'

'Take care of yourself, Sylvia.'

I don't reply. It's the end of the fairy tale. The beauty and the poet. The beauty, after all, has no brain and is determined to stretch her wings. I leave.

You used to glow? Well, now you can burn!

Ian is English, a very talented actor classically trained at the prestigious Royal Academy of Dramatic Art. He has acted alongside Richard Burton and John Hurt, been directed by Franco Zeffirelli . . .

He splits his time between Europe and the States. I would love to spend some time there, I've never done more than pass through. Going to Hollywood, living a passionate life there, with Ian, trying my luck. He will help me.

Ian's career has reached a plateau that according to him doesn't reflect his talent. It's the truth. His agent tells me that if he'd been three inches taller he would have had as glittering a career as Sean Connery. This state of affairs frustrates him, makes him explosive. I become the passive receptacle of his moods. I represent the injustice and fickleness of the profession. I'm an untrained, accidentally successful actress, yet I outstrip him in everything – height as well as the fuss I still provoke, my continuing popularity.

Ian's resemblance to French singer Sacha Distel is striking. The public confirms this – often when I'm managing to walk through an airport or down the street disguised and unnoticed, we hear: 'Sacha! Sacha!'

Ian thunders: 'I can't believe these idiots!' He yells out: 'Stop it!'

He makes up for his rages with a great deal of charm. Ian is very versatile. He can drench me in feminine sweetness after having been quite brutal. It's when he's worn out and exhausted that he's tender. He weeps sometimes, regretting his fits and spitefulness. Then he's on the attack again, for no reason, raining down on me like a hailstorm.

'Look at you! You don't know how to act! You can't even speak and walk at the same time! You don't understand anything, you don't do anything! You're not an actress, just a pretty clothes horse, just lucky! All you've got is luck and a nice arse!'

I look away. Cruelty is inflicting hatred on someone who craves your love. I long for this handsome actor to tell me that I'm even slightly talented. But he can't. Talent belongs to him only, it's his prerogative, his survival, not to be shared.

Sometimes I cry, wounded, hurt to the quick in my weakest spot. Then I rally, and yell. It's easy.

'Look, I *can* speak while walking!' I retort. 'Look at me! I'm walking, coming towards you and speaking to you. You're a midget! A failure! Frustrated! Tiny! Just as nature made you!'

We scream, and sob, and break objects from our set, acting out a tragedy. Only our hatred of ourselves is real. I don't love myself, he doesn't love himself, we don't love each other. This is self-hatred, applied to the other.

Sometimes Ian stops as if someone's suddenly called 'Cut!' He grabs me by the waist, spins me round and tells me that I'm beautiful. He kisses me, caresses me and declaims: 'Forgive me, O beauty! Forgive me!' A fine performance from the Royal Academy of Dramatic Art. If I remain angry we do what we do best, make fierce love for hours; then, exhausted, my fire flickers and dies.

The next morning, Ian continues his attentions and pleas for forgiveness by generously and skilfully cooking a traditional English breakfast whose smell, colours and nourishing intention I adore.

The best thing about Ian? His 'bed and breakfast'! The eggs are scrambled with a little cream, the Harrods baked beans come in a subtle blood-red sauce, the toast is the best in London, and it's all served by a naked Ian.

The worst? Everything else.

Ian liked partying, and party fuels.

'How do you manage, staying up all night for days on end, drinking so heavily?'

Ian screams with laughter.

Drinking is something I do already, so that just carries on, I fit right in. But I also discover the innocent-looking white powder at the root of his frenzy. I stare, fascinated, at the snorters and their powder.

'It's coke. Do you want to try it?'

Is this really a drug? If it were dangerous would it be taken as openly and commonly as this? Surely it would show on people – they would fall ill, be hospitalised, unable to work or run their lives; they would be on drugs and everyone would know it.

No, cocaine seems the opposite of a drug, more of a super-vitamin, something very fashionable, not really dangerous, expensive, a stimulant that dilutes alcohol, a necessary fuel if you want to keep up.

I try it. In a Paris nightclub in the early hours, amid peals of laughter, strobe lighting, a massive disco ball, kisses in the shadows; amid great floods of words, sounds, alcohol. I initiate myself, mimicking, into the cocaine ritual on the smoked glass of a low table.

I take a tiny knob of the slightly sticky, detergent-like powder out of a transparent plastic bag. I cut through it with a dry teaspoon, and place half carefully back in its bag. With the back of the spoon I crush my little marble, flattening it until it looks like a stamp. The powder is dense, so fine that it's impossible to make out the individual grains. Then, with the edge of a credit card, I slice through the stamp to create long thin lines like strands of spaghetti, as equal and parallel as I can. I roll up a smooth new banknote, hold one nostril shut with my index finger and poke the note up the other. I follow the line, inhaling as hard as possible, like downing a drink in one, so that the powder travels far into my nose, close to the centre of my brain. The slightly bitter taste moves quickly into my throat – the powder has made its journey. The effect is immediate. An electric tingling, my eyes opening wide, the feeling of being perfectly, delightfully lucid, the desire to move and to talk. My brain sparkles and initially my stomach lurches in response. I'm a little afraid, I know instinctively that my body is being overridden, that this food is alien.

I will repeat this ritual every day, and then several times a day, for several years. I will become hooked, a multiple addict.

Cocaine will give me the illusion of being confident, sparkling, on top form, of being in control of my own life and that of other people. I will be unable to resist that illusion.

I powder my nose.

Cocaine and alcohol are a good match. The strength of the drug revives, it delays the slowing down, the fog, the loss of balance. Coke provokes in me an irresistible need to drink. I drink and I snort. I live from high to crash, crash to high. Very up, then very down – an artificially imposed manic depression. Ian and I engage in absurd one-upmanship and competition. Who can drink and snort the most? Who can hold out longest before collapsing?

Massive doses of cocaine give me intense paranoia, as well as a sudden awareness that I'm on the road to ruin, a panoramic perspective on my life and the mess I've made of it. I become incapable of moving, unable to leave my room; I want to be by myself, far from other people, the instigators of this trap and seekers of my downfall. I weep inconsolably for my helplessness, replaying the film of my life with my eyes closed. I watch the journey from child to star. The whole film. I am in a movie. I'm going to wake up, at home, in a country that suits me, inhabited by normal people, and start again at the beginning.

My career is still defined by the triumph of *Emmanuelle* and success of its sequel. My roles in 'normal' movies have not made much impact, but my career could still take off again.

*

We move to Los Angeles for a while, to try it out. My son comes too. I create a few lucid moments in every day to spend with Arthur. I duck under a cold shower, cry out, dry myself off vigorously and go to play with my son. I always force myself to be cheerful, lively and loving. I exercise to help my body manage the excesses, and so that I'm in good shape when I see my son, my respite, my joy.

My mother and sister take turns helping me. They let me live my life, not realising what's going on. They think me a little changed – overexcited, chatty, newly confident. They put it down to success, to the new country. My mother and sister keep their eyes shut. They don't understand my life, it's so different from theirs. They are impressed by this luxurious lifestyle, by the amount of leisure time I have and by my fawning entourage, although my mother does regularly express her view that this isn't the life for a child. She often says that Arthur would be better off living in Utrecht with her, peacefully, away from this circus. I don't listen.

Marianne enjoys herself in Los Angeles. She bustles about, getting her hair coloured, taking herself in hand. She swaps glasses for contact lenses – much more modern. She puts on make-up. My sister feels fine wherever she is, she adapts easily. She has moved from one city to another just as she left the hotel for our neighbours' house. She decides to learn to drive, to acquire that skill so necessary to life in LA, where the neighbourhoods are linked by motorway. My little sister is stepping into her freedom, emancipating herself.

'You should get your licence, too!'

My sister tries to convince me, wanting to bring me down to earth. Drive? Myself? No, I'd rather be driven, rather go where

I'm taken. I'll go anywhere, but I'll travel in style. Open the door for me please, sir ... what delightful glamour, what considerate attention! Special treatment for the lady! When I hear the door click softly shut I lie back languorously on the smooth leather, relaxing, unfurling under the beneficial effects of this thoughtfulness, this punctual acknowledgement.

Drive? ... I sit down pensively. No, I will never drive ... my mother was always driving, always exhausted. She had a terrible accident when I was a child. I was four years old, Marianne was little more than a baby.

'Do you remember Mum's accident?'

This is the first time I've dared to bring up this painful memory. Marianne doesn't reply.

My mother was pregnant with our brother Nicolas. She was working very hard. Exhaustion had hollowed her face and left dark rings under her eyes. She didn't sleep much, she found it hard to let go, into a reprehensible lack of activity. One night she was completely worn out and her eyes closed at the wheel. She was hurrying to a friend's birthday party, the kind of thing she rarely went to. I had stayed with my grandmother, but Marianne was in the car and the boot was full of wine for the party ...

The car rolled over several times and eventually came to an upright, smoking stop at the foot of a huge tree.

My mother regained consciousness a few hours later, in a hospital. A priest had left his little black case at the foot of her bed, containing a crucifix and everything he might need for the Extreme Unction.

She had injuries on her face and chest, and an arm and leg were broken. She was pale and fragile, but alive.

'What is that case?' she asked weakly.

'Don't speak please, just stay calm, the priest is coming.'

'I don't need a priest, I need a doctor! I'm alive!'

'Calm down, it's just a precaution. You seemed so weak – you lost a lot of blood, the impact was intense, and then all that alcohol could have killed you . . .'

'What alcohol? I never drink and drive.'

'The police report is categorical. A very strong smell of alcohol was coming from the car . . .'

'From the boot perhaps, but not from me! I need a doctor, I'm pregnant. Do you understand, I'm expecting a child!'

My mother put her hands on her belly, then suddenly stopped speaking. She straightened up her bandaged torso and looked all around, examining the room. She brought a hand to her mouth. Her eyes moistened and her lips twisted.

'Marianne! Where is my daughter?! Marianne!!!'

'Do stop yelling like that! What daughter? There is no daughter.'

There is no daughter.

'No daughter?! Marianne! Marianne! Marianne!'

My sister had disappeared without the slightest trace, except in my mother's memory. She had vanished without a whimper. Marianne was gone. She had flown out of the sunroof like an angel. My mother yelled loudly. It hurt. She tried to stand up despite her injuries, despite the bones poking out of her skin. My mother was experiencing a moment of pure terror. This was tragedy – violent, unreal tragedy; death too, perhaps, her daughter dead perhaps, because of her, through her own fault only, her weakness. It was unbearable. My mother kept screaming until her voice was nothing but a squeak, then fainted. My mother's voice, its journey from roar to murmur, echoed through Utrecht hospital for a very long time. A dissonant harmony, a mingled, hoarse, breathless cry: 'Marianne!' A cry of such pain that the nurse had never heard one like it. My mother screaming her suppressed love for my sister, for us; just once, once only, in a great flood, a long, vibrant cry.

The nurse explained what had happened to the police, who immediately returned to the scene of the accident. Marianne was found sitting on a high branch, her skull cracked, mute and covered in blood. After this, my sister developed a strong sense of insecurity. She sought instinctively to escape, and found refuge with the neighbours.

'That's ancient history, Sylvia! All women drive here, in California, all the stars – it's cool! Driving your own car is the latest thing.'

My sister is insistent. I bet she wants to see me subject to the challenges of reality.

'Is it? Really? Cool? Do you think so?'

I decide to get my licence out of spite. I'm the eldest!

The machine and I are innately and definitively incompatible. I don't know what to do with the levers, or when to do it. I am incapable of driving, but I'm proud. Marianne has got her licence so I'll get mine, with a few dollars and plenty of smiles.

Goodbye Emmanuelle will be shot in the Seychelles. Ian auditions to be my lover in the film. He is not hired because he doesn't speak French. The producers want a sleeker, younger man, not so assertive, with a perfect body. Jean-Pierre Bouvier is chosen. He is the embodiment of naivety, of pure desire.

Jean-Pierre sleeps with a photo of Gérard Philipe over his bed. This entertains me. Perhaps he's disappointed, dreaming of another role? He must have taken this as a springboard, just as I did. I sprang up very high, and bounced, but never landed where I had intended.

The Seychelles is a paradise. I know it's hardly original to say so, but nothing could be truer. Paradise as we dream of it, a raw, natural, pure Garden of Eden before the fall. The beauty of the Seychelles is alive, its land virginal, its sea more than transparent. My body regains its former vitality; it feels at home in this landscape and is reborn in the fresh air, as when I went on holiday to the Utrecht countryside as a young girl.

The wild and innocent Seychelles countryside is the setting for one of my loveliest erotic scenes: we make love in the water, a few feet from the shore. The movements of our bodies are diluted by the liquid element, the water flows over us, covers us, unites us. Like the body, the sea is in constant movement. Love like a wave . . . .

We are shooting in a magnificent villa belonging to the President of the Seychelles. I later discover the unofficial compensation for this loan: the President wants to watch the love scenes on the beach!

'Has he asked to watch the clothed scenes?' I ask.

The crew giggles.

'Well, tell the President that he won't see me clothed or naked. He can go to the cinema like everyone else!'

François Leterrier is a director, not a photographer. I enjoy the actor's task – being directed and moulded, making an effort, delving into the gap between reality and fantasy to become someone else. I like this other world, this forgetting of myself. The actor works in order to escape, not to find himself. You become an actor by leaving yourself, and then you have to keep acting. How tragic!

My French is almost fluent and my accent very faint. Leterrier likes my voice, but the production team decides to keep tradition with the earlier parts by having me dubbed again.

I am once more working with the lovely Alexandra Stewart. She will reappear regularly throughout my film career. We're friends, I enjoy her company. Alexandra is dreading the scene where we have to flirt and kiss each other passionately. Life is hilarious – I remind her of St-Germain-des-Prés, where she seemed so liberated, so carefree. She remembers, a little embarrassed. She was so young, she says, and drunk!

'Well, let's drink then!'

'Good idea!'

After a few glasses, we're laughing heartily at almost anything. I give her some advice:

'You have to forget everything – other people, the technicians, morality, your fear. Forget everything and look at me. We're the same. See only me, look into my eyes, look at my mouth, look at it. Think of my mouth as a joy you absolutely must taste. Be free, look at me, desire me . . .'

Alexandra looks very beautiful in a long black dress with a plunging neckline, her skin tanned. She's wearing a heavy necklace made from large creamy pearls. Her hair is combed back, her face turns to the light like a flower. Her eyes are luminous, brushed with silvery powder. Her lips are painted sienna. We're sitting on a sofa. I take her hand, which she gives me unenthusiastically. I move towards her, and she suddenly stops laughing. My lips are the closest part of me to her. I part my lips as if to drink, close my eyes. Alexandra is conquered. Her hand squeezes mine, our lips grab at each other playfully.

I always bring little souvenirs back from a film shoot, it's a habit of mine. A piece of pottery, spices, jewellery, a photo of a child, a kiss . . .

The tropical countryside continues my detoxification; I am protected by distance and in this paradise my life calms down.

Not for long. There's bad news: a Dutch tabloid has run the headline 'SYLVIA KRISTEL RAPED BY HER FATHER!'

Before leaving I had given an interview to a new Dutch tabloid. This paper was the first to fully understand the public's insatiable interest in the private lives of celebrities, and had been causing quite a stir. The journalist was pleasant, reassuring, sly. He asked me about my childhood, which no one knew about. I can't remember what state I was in, it's all a blur. What did I say? I remember crying when he asked about my father. Crying is for me a rare and immodest act, my cracked heart leaking a little. I don't like crying on-screen, it's too intimate. I sometimes feel that if I start crying I will be haemophiliac, unable to stop. When I cry I drink, at least as much as I'm crying, trying to refill my punctured heart. But escape knows no boundaries, and when I drink, I don't stop. I keep going until I forget why I am crying, until I forget everything. I can remember speaking about 'Uncle' Hans and my little girl's peep show. I wanted to talk about that forgotten, never-spoken event, to explain who I was, to destroy the fairy tale. But the journalist didn't give a damn about 'Uncle' Hans, it wouldn't sell. The amalgam was quickly achieved and the scandal printed – 'my father raped me'.

Everyone is shattered. My father, his wife, my mother, me. The news makes every TV channel. I make a public denial but the damage is already done. My stepmother accuses me of having lied in a bid for publicity, and starts an appalling process of blackmail. She wants her slice of the pie, and will lodge a complaint unless I buy her a new Mercedes. My mother is distressed out of love for my father. I feel abused all over again. The idea that I could have lied about my father's nature in a quest for extra attention sickens me; I am devastated.

I don't want this idyllic shoot to end. My father won't speak to me, my stepmother is raining insults on me and my mother would rather forget the whole sorry story.

The rejection is unbearable. I have run out of coke but alcohol is easy to find, despite being in a Muslim country. So I drink, and dance, and drink, and howl.

I like the scene where – face to camera, an extreme close-up on my face and eyes – I seem possessed, incandescent. The fire was real.

56

We end up in the law courts. My stepmother sues the news-paper and me for defamation. I sue the paper myself, in self-defence. I go to the journalist's office to try for a friendly resolution. He suggests driving me to the court where the hearing will take place. I accept and find myself, not having realised the absurdity of the situation, sitting in the car of the sole accused just as my father's ancient convertible Mercedes arrives. He is frozen and sad, sitting in the passenger seat. My stepmother is driving, still running the show. My father doesn't see me, he is absent, forced to emerge from his retire-ment for a sordid matter he doesn't understand. He must by order of law say that no, he didn't rape his daughter, his secret princess, his pretty figurine. I am ashamed. I would have liked to swap cars, to lift up his chin and tell him that all this is the fault of other people, not us. That we're seeing the worst side of human nature but we'll get through it. I would have pushed back the roof with a creaking of canvas, the sun would have burst through and we would have left, just the two of us, free amid a deafening mechanical racket.

The newspaper was convicted and my father given com-pensation. *Goodbye Emmanuelle* was a success, but again less so than the previous film. The French release of *The Joys of a Woman* had been so delayed by the censorship board and

the lawsuit that it only came out in January 1978, just six months before *Goodbye*. The public was a little wearied by this quick succession – and yet the final part is perhaps the most accomplished and beautiful: subtle and stunningly erotic. Serge Gainsbourg wrote the music and the lyrics, with their clever, explicit play on words: *'Emmanuelle loves caresses manual and oral ... Emmanuelle loves intellectuals and workers manual ...'*

I like this handsome Serge; he, Ian, Jane Birkin and I hang out together. I like his genius, his artful drinking, the way he destroys himself as he creates, consciously, as if sacrifice were indispensable to the unbearable nature of life.

Jacques Itah negotiates on my behalf a contract with the all-powerful Universal Pictures. Business is rolling on. Soon I'll land a lead role in a big-budget international film with a superb cast. Ian is jealous and says so; he is irritable, unsatisfied, unpredictable.

In LA I meet Ian's American agent Elaine Rich. I immediately hit it off with this little Slavic-origin woman, a pale Russian doll, a Jewish New Yorker with a warm, loving heart sustained by inner dynamism, who erupts into my life and work at exactly the right moment. She decides to take on my American career, which she thinks can move up a gear.

She wants to introduce me to some producer friends.

'They're sending a limousine, darling!'

'But I've just bought a new car; I want to show off my driving!'

---

* Translation (McLean) of Gainsbourg's original: *'Emmanuelle aime les caresses manuelles et buccales ... Emmanuelle aime les intellectuels et les manuels ...'*

'Are you sure?'

'Come on, let's go!'

I've bought myself a Pacer, a kind of modern bug, with huge windows. Very fashionable. Driving is fun, and I'm in a good mood. Bring on the producers!

Elaine is strangely silent and huddled. I'm sure I'm driving properly but Elaine seems frightened. OK, so I am zigzagging a little – I've had a few drinks, as before every important appointment – but I'm managing to drive in a more or less straight line. On one of LA's tentacle highways I start telling Elaine how grateful and happy I am that she's looking out for me like this, giving me this new opportunity.

'That's right, darling, but do concentrate. Honey, I beg you, concentrate!'

'But you don't realise, in this job it's so rare to be able to count on –'

'Here! Right! Take this exit!'

Elaine is waving her arm around and pointing at the road sign.

'This one?'

'Yes! Get off here!'

I blink; I'm not wearing my glasses. Oh yes, it is the right name on the sign, but it's all going too fast, I'm going to miss the exit.

'Turn off, for the love of God! We're going to LA, not Santa Barbara! Turn off!'

Action! With a great heft of the steering wheel I move from the left-hand lane to the right, cutting almost horizontally across the middle two. A huge, gleaming truck blasts its steamship horn, barely covering the screams of Elaine, who is

The cabin hardly bobs around at all; I feel suspended, as if in a soft, white metal hammock, sliding through the peaceful, sunny sky on the silvery arc I imagine linking Paris to Hollywood. The clouds are rootless mountains forming and re-forming – snow, bubbles, giant candyfloss glistening in the oblique sun.

The air hostess's hairstyle is immaculate. She smiles at me, steadfast and devoted. She fills me with Dom Perignon. I am in the clouds, higher than the sky, in heaven.

What's the weather like down there, at sea level, tulip level? How strong is the wind? What day is it? I count the shadows playing on the sea, then close my eyes against the blinding light and drink, filling my void.

I would like to bathe in this sky, to dive into the mother-of-pearl, naked, wrapping myself in these soft bubbles.

I stand up to climb the narrow spiral staircase – a showgirl's prop – to the open bar. I sashay, putting on a show for my own benefit. I am alone, facing a deserted and well-stocked bar. A nice big glass of vodka and I dance; a little bitter powder and I dance some more, alone and free, sure of myself. The alcohol goes to my head and slows my dance. I slip over, kneel up, laugh; some more bitter powder snorted directly off the floor and I stand up and dance once more. Then I go back down the stairs, sit, cross my naked, pale pink legs at the thigh and press the button. A soft 'ding-dong' and the air hostess will arrive, reliably, each time I press. My mouth is half open, I am chewing my lip. I smile so I don't have to talk, reach out my arm, its glass extension is filled. I drink.

I haven't slept and LA is here already. The plane lands, everything sparkles here, even the night.

'Good evening, Miss Kristel. Did you have a nice flight?'

The driver is on time, standing tall just in front of me with his Universal sign. Young, handsome, with a candid white smile – I am definitely in LA. He puts out his hand to take my bags; I keep the case and give him my hand. I squeeze it hard; I am exhausted and remote. I walk erratically, following the driver who guides me through this foreign maze. Nothing is familiar to me and yet this is where I live, my exiled land, my place of work.

LA is a town for hard work, for effort, for believing in the dream and shining and then leaving. Everyone leaves LA a little burnt, prematurely aged, on the 'wrong side of the hill' as the Americans say – when you're thirty years old.

I am amazed at all these women trying to hold back time in a town where it passes faster and more intensely than anywhere else, where the sparkles are in fact rough scales that graze.

In this town women mutilate themselves incessantly, too closely involved to realise what they're doing. Pointless – leave the swollen lips and porcelain complexions on the surgeons' tables! There's no point in fighting; they will always see through your mask to the age beneath. You will be made to pay heavily for past desire. Your birth certificate will be produced, crassly, like a branded registration number. You will be told that you are well preserved. You will be jeered at in the papers, and behind your back. Vengeance will be widespread and massive, as ferocious as you were once beautiful.

hanging on to the ceiling handle with both hands. We make the turn-off.

That was my first meeting with Menahem Golan and Yoram Globus. As we left Elaine – satisfied and calmer now – said: 'Shall we take a taxi? You're a real star, darling, you need a lifelong chauffeur.'

A few days later, after stalling it yet again, I abandon my car on Sunset Boulevard. I can't manage the coordination. I'll be singing away and forget to work the clutch when I brake and accelerate. I've had enough of this untameable car. I leave the keys with a shopkeeper I know.

'Someone will come by for them, I'm going home on foot!'

Ian knows everyone in Hollywood, and we are invited to all the parties. The Californian dress code is very casual – I was expecting stars in evening dresses but they all wear jeans and light, revealing cotton tops, their skin always a little burnt by this constant sun. No jeans or plunging necklines for me. On the contrary, the more buttoned and covered up I am the better I feel. I wear head to toe Chanel. I look like an alien, and why not?

The famous actor who greets us is of course surprised by my designer armour.

'Was your friend expecting me naked?!' I whisper in Ian's ear; he finds his friend's reaction amusing.

'Of course, darling. He was expecting Sylvia Kristel at her very best!'

'Bastard!'

A great start to the evening.

I decide to enjoy myself, and wander around checking the place out.

Warren Beatty is looking fantastic, all in black. His eyes are roaming, getting a sense of the territory, and it's not hard to see that I'm among the potential prey. I smile at him and Ian leads me away – predators always sniff each other out.

I stand and admire the fabulous, magnetic singer with her unique laugh, long curly hair and white linen flapping in the hilltop breeze. The house is extraordinary, with views on both sides: a massive horizon of slightly rough, dark blue ocean streaked with fine white lines, and then the night-time city stretching out as far as the eye can see, dotted with blinking lights, a dark, tackily sparkling monster.

'You're not swimming?' asks our host, pointing to the enormous, limpid pool in which a few pretty, near-naked starlets are already thrashing around, giggling and asking for help taking off their burdensome swimsuits. A few men join them, fully dressed.

'No thank you, I'm a little cold . . .'

It must be thirty degrees on this lovely summer evening and my Chanel suit is buttoned up to the neck, but it's true, I am a little cold. It must be this constant wind, or else loneliness.

Ian has vanished. I start looking for him inside the villa's several wings – a maze of rooms through which I venture limply, goblet in hand. Some of the doors are open, others not. I push at them as I did at the hotel, and each opens on a different scene. A bare-chested man crashed out asleep, two others snorting, and then a young, naked mermaid on dry land, being fucked at the heart of a joyful and grunting little group – a most familiar tableau. I close the door and continue. A famous rock star is shooting up on the floor; he glances at me, trembling slightly, his long hair sticky with sweat and obscuring his slightly rolling eyes. He looks like he's having a good time; I leave him to it. I don't find Ian. Still knocking back the champagne I return to the swimming-pool area, where Warren Beatty introduces himself pleasantly and congratulates me on my most European elegance. I thank him and carry on walking. I guzzle this cold champagne. Champagne is all I want. I breathe in the cool night air and hum the song that gets me moving as soon as I hear it; fresh, sensual, rhythmical, played over and over again and each time sending the same wave of pleasure through the crowd of guests. Donna Summer sings, '*Baby, I want you now . . . now . . . come into my arms . . .*' This song, 'Could it be Magic', has an electric effect on me and I can't help dancing. '*Baby, I want you now . . . now . . .*' Her voice is hoarse, pleading, Donna Summer is on fire, singing of feminine arousal and desire, the pace of pleasure building to a crescendo. It's a hymn to modern love, the best song of the seventies. I dance dreamily: '*Baby, I want you now . . . Now! Come into my arms, let me know the wonder above you . . .*'

On the way home Ian and I argue, giving each other a hard time for disappearing – and yet I know *I* was there. When we get back I pour myself a large cognac and finish the lines left on the coffee table, with disco music blaring. Ian goes off to bed. I will collapse in the lounge a few hours later, and be woken by my sister.

The parties are many, similar: I snort, slip on my silk-lined Chanel clothes, drink and fall over.

'Sylvia, I want to live in Holland. I'm going back, with Arthur,' says Marianne.

She is serious, rather sombre. She gives reasons for this proposition, or decision. She explains, as my mum has, that this isn't the life for a child, that she loves Arthur so much, that he'll be better off in Europe with her and our mother. He may be far away, but he will wait for me. He'll understand that I'm working, he'll go to school like a normal child and will be enveloped in my sister's and mother's redoubled affection ... Marianne is insistent. I find myself unable to reply. Ian doesn't like having my son around. Marianne begs me to agree.

'You're right, take Arthur and go ...'

I don't remember having been sad. In fact I was pleased, relieved that my son was escaping from that life, my life, my fog. I'd go back, I'd try to, just as soon as I could.

We're going out this evening. My hairdresser and make-up artist have come over. It's another big Malibu party at another actor's house. I want to look beautiful. Ian protests, saying that I'm trying too hard, I'm not with the programme, in California people only dress up for the Oscars. I don't give a damn. I'm a European film star, I come from a refined continent, I'm different and I want everyone to know it!

Several hours spent in front of the mirror, beautifying. I have a lovely, perfectly lacquered chignon. My eyelids are powdered in a gradation of silvers, my lips painted a shiny red and I am wearing a new cream silk dress. I like what I see. I smile at myself, congratulating myself because no one else is. Champagne! I prepare an ice bucket in the lounge, plunge the pretty bottle into it and sit down, mirror in hand, to inspect the

58

The Wilshire Hotel, Hollywood's palace. The permanent, uniform blue of the sky makes you feel as if you're on a film set. It's a very luxurious place.

'Mr Delon's room, please.'

'Who wants to see him?'

'Sylvia Kristel.'

'Wait a moment, please. I'll tell him you're here ... Yes, Mr Dello is expecting you.'

I smile. We are not famous here – neither he nor I. Anonymity, a step backwards, one's name repeated. Even the European tourists aren't interested. They are distracted, on an adventure, they dreamed about me in Europe and nowhere else. *Eurotrash* is the name given by Americans in the business to actors from the Old Continent trying to break into Hollywood. Trash is something you throw away, something you don't need, used up and worn out. Charming. I used to think they were waiting for me, that my exotic charm would hypnotise this puritanical continent. I was wrong.

I go upstairs to see *Mr Dello*, that legendary, anonymous actor. A dialogue coach opens the door to the suite and greets me; Alain Delon will be with us in a moment. I flash a wide smile, and make sure to walk in a straight line – I've had a few drinks. I am intimidated and a little anxious. Delon has played opposite the top actresses; what will he think of me? I've never found anything better than alcohol to take the edge off shyness and nerves. I suck my extra-strength, tongue-burning mint and sit down.

The coach reads me the script:

'*Would you like a coffee, sir?*'

'*Yes please, Miss.*'

'*Espresso? With sugar?*' etc.

He asks me to repeat it, wanting to hear my accent. I burst out laughing and reply that, given the complexity of the text in this first scene, I can do without his services. I would rather be alone with the handsome actor, to get to know him, and anyway I don't like rehearsing. My work is natural, instinctive. I don't rehearse.

The coach leaves. Delon arrives. I shake his hand. He is surprised by the absence of the coach, and unimpressed by my initiative. The room is huge. Delon paces restlessly up and down, irritated and ignoring me. I stand to leave but he holds me back.

'Run me a bath!' he says with authority.

A male authority, physical and natural, brooking no argument. I go into the bathroom and run the water. The tub is large and as round as a basin. The bubbles rise and the steam dampens my forehead. I return to the room, where Delon stares at me insistently. He is bare-chested, his shirt on the floor. There he stands in the middle of the room, looking at me, not saying anything.

What does he want? The obvious? No, I can feel his confusion. He is oscillating between desire and disgust, longing and contempt, and each moment that passes worsens his hesitation and my discomfort. What is his pleasure? Where is his joy? His gaze is clouded, his mind busy, his hands rubbing and clasping each other. He is beautiful, and nearly naked. Does he want to play, to kill time? I think of the other women who have stood before him. What did they do, faced with this body? Who resisted, who understood him? More than pleasure, he wants the control of pleasure. More than to give he wants to promise, to see desire in the texture of my skin, on my lips, to examine my desire and then deny it, deny me. Does he need this denial in order to exist? Does he want to control his desire, or to risk it? I don't know. Uncertain, I do not refrain. It wouldn't make sense to resist, I have never seen such beauty and darkness combined in one man. Every curve, every burgeoning smile is a promise whose effect – pleasant or damaging – one cannot know. From this unknown is born my compelling desire. I move closer, unbutton my blouse, I want to play too. I want to know, to climax or burn, to rediscover contempt, ambiguous love, arousal. My fingers slide along my skin. Delon is watching them. My breasts stretch towards him, offering two buds from beneath the fabric. I gaze at the handsome actor with total neutrality, concealing my desire and allowing my fingers to move as if they had a mind of their own. I let my arms hang down at my sides, my blouse slips off with exquisite slowness, I am nearly naked, too. Delon looks at the limp cotton on the floor as at a trophy; he waits, gaze downturned, then looks up suddenly. He has decided. He points quickly at my blouse and says to me: 'You can get dressed and go.'

I bump into Delon on the first day of the shoot. I avoid his gaze. He doesn't give a damn and immediately asks me: 'Can I see your trailer?'

'If you want . . .'

We go there straight away. He looks into my mobile dressing room and mutters angrily: 'Yeah . . . it's no better.'

'What's the matter?'

'Don't you understand anything? Can't you see these are shitty trailers? They're taking the piss out of me!'

He stalks off, furious.

The director's trailer is larger and more comfortable than his. Delon takes it over, ejecting its occupant almost by force. In this jungle, Delon calls the shots. He wants respect, and he will get it.

The embarrassed director complains to the producer, as if reporting Delon to a teacher. The producer tells him pleasantly to shut it. Delon is the star, there must have been a mistake in the allocations, Delon is right.

Delon doesn't speak to me for the rest of the shoot. *The Concorde: Airport '79* is one of the last disaster films made by Universal. The genre has caught up with the film: it is a disaster.

Delon refuses to kneel before me as the script demands. He is, however, contractually obliged to do so. The scene hasn't changed. Is it so humiliating to kneel before me? The crew is all aflutter, some back him up . . . it wouldn't be good for his image. Is that so? Delon procrastinates for a few hours, he knows he's got to do it but this constraint is unbearable for a free man who has won or snatched his freedom.

Delon is massively tense when he does the scene, which paralyses me.

I am timid, small.

Later, I regret not having played his game myself. I would have taken my shoe off slowly, lifted my leg, bent my knee, put my foot on his head and twiddled my toes on the prostrate man. I would have crushed him, just for a laugh, just to see. Perhaps he would do that scene now? He seems softer, older, his demons calmed.

Delon was extremely tense. He wasn't bad, but trapped, careful, anxious, suspicious. He used to snap in self-defence, protecting himself. I sensed in this man with the intense gaze a never-admitted pain that ate away at him. He was complex to say the least, vulnerable and powerful, at his own mercy, that most handsome of traps, a magnificent and broken being.

Towards the end of the shoot the director starts being overtly misogynistic. He treats me badly, shouting, making me repeat things all the time for no reason.

I have had another physical fight with Ian – over nothing, I can't even remember what. Of course, I 'bumped into a cupboard'. My left eye is a little swollen, the lid purple, the make-up artist does her best without asking questions.

One criticism too many from the director and I crack, give in, burst into tears; it's too much, too much hostility aimed at me. Delon sees me trembling in the corner and comes to me gently. At last. Without a word he stretches out his hand and takes my child's hand, firmly and tenderly. I understand that it's going to be OK now, that he will be kind, as deep down he is.

The rest of the shoot goes fine.

59

That is when I should have left Ian; things had gone too far.

The hatred he sometimes throws at me has unknown roots. I am unable to think, unable to leave, I just keep going.

Elaine warns me, she knows Ian well. He is a very talented actor but tortured, egocentric, misogynous. He can be cruel – that's just how it is. She tells me the tale of the scorpion and the dog. A scorpion asks a stray dog to help it cross the river. The dog agrees, but makes the scorpion promise not to sting. The scorpion climbs on the dog's back and the dog swims across the river. Once on solid ground, the scorpion stings the dog. The dog asks: 'Why did you do that?' and the scorpion replies: 'I couldn't help myself.'

I do my best, I earn money, feed the people around me, and give to other people – my loved ones, the public – the care I struggle to give myself.

I receive a lot of mail, some of it surprising. People thank me for helping them maintain desire in their marriages.

Ian is right, I don't make art. But I entertain well. Art? That will come a bit later in my life. I will find my artistic expression – more intimate even than nudity – in painting.

I won't sit on my rattan throne in the pantheon of cinematic art, but I will perhaps linger in people's memories. I have never claimed anything more. You have to accept what you are.

There's a real sweetness to thinking that one can live on in memories, that after I am dead, cremated, I will remain a siren-ghost in people's minds. One sunny spring Sunday I will suddenly be reborn on a plasma screen, impertinent and care-free, a young woman of twenty with fevered gaze and obscene hand. Desire may outlive me.

I argue frequently with Ian; our bond is weakened but still holds. It is founded on powerful physical attraction and a common interest. It's a passionate, fantastical relationship; we don't love each other; on the contrary, we detest each other. Hate may be the opposite of love but they are both full of obsession, suffering and excess.

I live with Ian for almost five years. That's how long it takes me to hit rock bottom, to reject the unacceptable and thus begin to respect myself.

I am pregnant. I'm glad. I will keep this child. Ian doesn't express an opinion, it's of no interest to him, I can do what I like. I tell the news to my mother and sister, who are doubtful. Will I be able to bring up a second child when I barely see my son? I tell them that it's an opportunity, a sign. I am going to change my life. The notion of aborting is unbearable to me. I accept the flow of life, the good and the bad; my son is the best thing in my life, I will keep this other child.

We spend a few months in London. Ian is filming and I go along too. During a visit to Paris I arrange to see a specialist. I am not managing to drink any less, and can sense that my body is finally starting to suffer. The whites of my eyes are turning yellow, I am alcoholic, pregnant, not yet thirty and at the end of my tether. I spend a whole day in detailed tests at a clinic. I try not to drink, for these few hours at least, but I can't. I have hidden a flask of cognac in my bag. My breath smells of mint, as it has for the last ten years.

The pleasant specialist consultant asks me to sit down so he can explain my test results. I watch his face for clues. Nothing.

'I'll explain the situation to you, Miss,' he says calmly. 'It's very simple. This test is a graded assessment, from 0 to 3. Zero indicates a liver which has never processed any alcohol. 3 means death from cirrhosis in under six months. Yours is 2.5.'

I start shaking. I had never thought I might die. Never. I am excessive, dependent, trapped, I am doing what my father did, and my mother, but I want to stay alive.

'You must stop straight away. Not one drop, lots of water and follow the treatment I will prescribe for you. I want to see you again in six months. If you follow my instructions, you should return to a score between 1 and 2.'

'I'll be back in six weeks, in good health.'

I make this promise as a challenge – that's the only way for me to manage, out of pride. I tell Ian about my tests, my resolutions. He says that I'll never do it. I will.

Arthur has come to visit, with my sister. I spend time with him. I teach him some little things – precautions, dangers, politeness, cleanliness. He tries hard, doing each gesture as I do, copying me. He's enjoying himself. I brush my teeth so he brushes his teeth. I finish my plate of vegetables, he does too. I go to the toilet, he follows me. It's his clever little way of saying: 'Watch out, Mum, take care of yourself – I'm going to be copying everything you do.'

'Remember to pull the chain, Arthur, and wash your hands!'

The message surpasses my intentions. He loves pulling the

chain, and does it for no reason except the sound of the water and the repetition of this adult gesture of which he is so proud. Arthur is at the age where he wants to be just like the grown-ups. He is becoming a big, clean boy who sometimes walks into an occupied toilet just to pull the chain. It makes me laugh. Marianne protests, gently.

I am more than three months pregnant, and haven't drunk for a few weeks. An eternity. I measure my alcohol dependence by the violence of the withdrawal that sometimes doubles me over, making me shake and cry out. I drink Coca-Cola, Perrier, tea, coffee, any liquid with a strong or fizzy enough taste to trick my palate. I can't stand flat water.

Ian doesn't change his habits one bit. He even mocks me, laughing and offering me a drink. It's too much, this is total disrespect. One night I fiercely reject this constant, lacerating contempt that I've been accepting out of passion, admiration and self-disgust. I answer back as hard as I can, my ferocity is real, I am beside myself. We fight, and scream. My son and Marianne are asleep. I lose my balance and fall down the stairs. My sister comes running, shrieking, and helps me up. Ian carries on yelling. I reassure my sister: I haven't broken anything, I fell like a stuntwoman, my skin is thicker than one might think. A few more bruises to add to my collection and that will be that. Luckily Arthur didn't wake up and have to see that.

The next day on the toilet I feel a piece of flesh slip out of me. I know what it is. I want to see. Looking down between my thighs I see a handful of blood, of unknown floating matter. I look away immediately, clapping my hand over my mouth; I won't scream, my son is just there behind the door, I can hear him. The door opens and he comes in.

'I'm going to pull the chain, Mummy!'

I smile at him – a mother's reflex – and bend double where I'm sitting, rolling into a ball, hiding myself. I let him do his adult thing. I hear the sound of the water, the little racket that makes Arthur laugh and washes away my horror and shame.

I am in revolt. If Arthur hadn't come in, and if Ian had been there I might have picked up the thing and thrown it at its father's face. He would have seen the destruction, would have had to believe in it. Yes, I would have done that.

Marianne holds me, and takes me to the hospital, saying I need to be examined and watched over in case I haemorrhage. She also tells Ian. It's the end of the shoot, he's organising the wrap party and is sorry but he won't be able to come.

I stay in hospital for two days, with only Marianne for company. Then I go back to the apartment, get my things and my son and leave for Paris without a word.

Ian turns up a few days later, pleading to see me. He begs me to return to London with him, to forgive him one last time. His act is stunning – the actor has completely taken over the man. Each word rings incredibly true and yet it is all false.

I feel dizzy. The stunt is almost perfect; it could give rise to feelings. I resist. Let the handsome actor perform his act elsewhere. I applaud his masterly performance slowly and heavily. My face is impassive, I say nothing, I'm still in pain. I demand that he leave.

As soon as Ian slams the door I feel both shattered and relieved. One more forgiveness would have permanently rubbished my tiny remaining pinch of self-esteem. I have managed to retain this atrophied, surviving part; it's a cutting with the potential for regrowth.

I return to the specialist doctor two months after my previous visit. I surprise him – my liver is recovering.

My miscarriage has traumatised me. I never want to live through that again, never. It has put a definitive stop to my maternal urges. I mustn't have another child. I suddenly decide to have my tubes tied, an operation usually reserved for prostitutes and mothers of large families. My mother and sister agree that it's a good idea, saying they couldn't bring up any more of my children. I undergo the operation in Los Angeles, with Marianne for company. As we leave the clinic I ask her to give me some time alone. I walk around Beverly Hills for hours. My sunglasses are huge, it's the fashion. They mask a dull but stubborn sadness. The goddess of love has been sterilised.

I move house – I'm changing set.

60

The lobby of the building is panelled in rare, red-veined pink marble, with big facing mirrors that produce infinite reflections. The sky is a flawless blue and the air warm as I return home to my new apartment in Colonial House, West Hollywood – one of Los Angeles' smartest neighbourhoods. The doorman greets me and opens the door. He knows me now, I'm his darling. He tries to chat – he's a real old-fashioned busybody. I do sometimes listen to him dishing the dirt on all the characters that live in this luxurious building. I rarely have time, and pretend to be above such gossiping, but actually I love these anecdotes, these trivial events that reveal people as they really are. I retain the curiosity of someone who grew up in a hotel, I still want to know what goes on behind closed doors, what the world doesn't see, I'm still intrigued by these sleek people and their rumpled, stained sheets.

I rush to the lift, smiling apologetically. I wait for a few moments while the machine descends to collect me from the ground floor. Behind me the front door opens again.

'Hello, Miss . . .'

The doorman offers his arm to the lady, wedging the door open with his foot.

'Leave me alone! You're very kind. But open your eyes, can't you?' The lady pats her thigh with her hand. 'Look! I've two legs, and a brain. For as long as my brain works I shall retain control of these wretched legs.'

I know this rasping, well-used voice. The diction is perfect and the accent refined.

The elderly, slow-moving, ramrod-straight lady climbs the three wide steps up to the lift with a dull groan, cursing the slowness that burdens her, one hand on the copper guard rail and the other on her patent leather handbag.

I am in the lift, and out of respect keep my finger on the button so the door stays open.

The lady enters, is surprised to see me, and immediately looks away.

The doorman once told me that she only takes the lift when it's empty. She must not have seen me, and can't back out now that she's in.

The lady is peering into the mirror, stretching her mouth vertically and horizontally. By pushing out her jaw she smooths the skin of her face and the folds of her mouth, then uses a finger to correct a fault in the shape of her lips – a section of the red outline has run at the corner. Letting her thick, tinted glasses slip down, her nose right against the mirror, she checks with enormous eyes that her lipstick is perfect. She casts an irritated glance at my obvious curiosity and regains her pose, unruffled, flawlessly upright. She stands stock-still, as frozen as a wax statue. The confined space fills with the familiar smell of alcohol blended with a sweet, heady, exclusive and feminine scent.

'Sixth floor; to the top, please! To the penthouse!'

There's an innate fury in each of her movements, a tired but still vibrant rage that suddenly animates an arm, or her face, and then stops. This tiny, frail lady is constantly readjusting her stiff body with just a hint of a grimace, snarling as she tugs at her Chanel suit or pats her perfectly blow-dried brown wig. She is a stylish, exasperated rebel, always in a rush. I know who she is, of course. Everyone in the building – and all over the world – knows who she is. Her strong, slim body has taken up a great deal of space; she is a giant, a monster who feeds on life and air, rarefied and electric. Will she remain silent? Or scream that this machine is too slow, that she's found out about me, that I'm nothing but a little naked strumpet? I am intimidated. I don't dare move. She senses this and turns her head slightly so she can see me without looking at me; this youthful emotion entertains her. I check her out more closely, the corners of her eyes, the roots of her artificial hair, the eye-lashes lengthened and weighed down with a young woman's mascara, the bright red nails that match her mouth. The hat perched on the back of her head is immaculate, the feather combed and gleaming. Everything is under control. The lift goes up with the faint sound of well-oiled machinery. It is modern, and moves smoothly. The number of each storey flashes as the red light moves towards the penthouse. At the first floor we hear Michel Polnareff playing his piano; the lady sighs and stamps her foot.

'He never stops! That's enough, Frenchie!'

Then she laughs, frankly, giving herself a moment's respite before gluing her face to the mirror once more, stretching out her mouth to correct the tiny damages inflicted on her lipstick by the angry words.

I don't get out at the second floor, where I live; I hold my breath, following her. When we get to the top floor the lady turns towards me and laughs, then gets hold of herself again and gives me a dry wave. The door has barely opened before she is leaving the lift, stepping forward slowly but precisely. A devoted, respectful woman is waiting at the door of the apartment and rushes to offer her arm for support.

'That's enough! I've two legs and a brain! More than one can say for you, Dorothy! You're useless! No one was waiting for me when I came out of the hairdresser, I had to take a cab!'

'But the driver was trying to find you, Miss Davis.'

'That driver is hopeless. I'm not exactly hard to recognise – the only wrinkled woman in Hollywood!'

'You're not wrinkled, Miss Davis, you're expressive –'

'Enough, Dorothy! Stop it!'

The doors close on a myth, a powerful, luminous star of the Hollywood galaxy, a woman devoured by her art, burnt, alone, magical. Bette Davis is the star of the building, and her quarrels with her assistant are a regular and joyful source of entertainment.

Miss Davis often steps out onto the balcony to watch for her slave's departure from the building, tracking her with a hosepipe she can barely control. A heavy jet of water from the top floor lands on the woman; she flees, emitting high-pitched little shrieks, while the drunken diva's loud, deep, throaty laugh resounds through the courtyard, interspersed with some very colourful language. When the assistant has disappeared from sight Miss Davis starts on the first-floor musician, the 'hippy crank', shouting 'Enough! Enough, Frenchie!' as she floods her balcony and screams with laughter.

I love this chic, lively, starry place.

*

Hugo pays me a friendly visit. He knows that I'm single and don't find it easy. He is passing through LA and invites himself over.

The Delon film wasn't a success. I'm not feeling confident about my career. I will stay in the States for one or two more films, and then return home. I am foundering in this world of commercial film, I'd like to do nothing but paint. Hugo encourages me. He tells me I should turn my apartment into a studio, clearing a big, pure space that would inspire me to create. He helps me move out the furniture, which we leave on the pavement. I keep the huge sofa, my soft nest and essential refuge. I continue painting, my other venture, the one that will age well and never come to an end.

In 1981 I have the second biggest success of my career, perhaps even my most successful financially, with an entertaining erotic film called *Private Lessons*, by Alan Myerson. It takes more than 50 million dollars in the United States alone. I don't know exactly how much profit was made with *Emmanuelle*. Unfortunately I wasn't paid in royalties – only the producer, Jaeckin and the scriptwriter got a cut proportional to the film's success, which is to say huge! I'm told that Jean-Louis Richard is still living off my Thai escapades.

I am pleased about this new success, but it goes almost unnoticed in France. I share my frustrations with Elaine:

'So it seems I'll never be recognised as a real actress . . .'

'But, darling, you're better than an actress, you're a goddess of love! In Hollywood there are more actresses than palm trees!'

'Do you think I have talent?'

'What a question! There's no success without talent. You have the talent to make people dream, you touch men and women in the very core of desire. Desire is vital, *you* are vital!'

Elaine has the knack of making you believe what she says, in a world where the prevailing paranoia stems from the genuine impossibility of trusting anyone. Everybody can legitimately be accused of manipulation, improper use of seduction, envy, and using their loved ones as tools and stepping stones. Everybody wants to shine – a little, a lot, as much as humanly possible! Americans have that sense of commodification: show business is the best possible word to describe the world in which I lived.

I trust Elaine, and I am right to. She protects me, and negotiates everything for me down to the last detail: the amount of time needed for my make-up, to keep my complexion young and fresh; the Dom Perignon; the bowl of fruit she insists I eat.

'Fruit, darling, lots of fruit!'

And peanut butter! Peanut butter is her miracle cure. Whenever Elaine thinks me skinny or depressed she prescribes thickly spread peanut butter toast.

'It's so nourishing!'

And I eat – not because I like the awful bland mush, but out of love for Elaine. Whenever I spot the big pot she carries around everywhere I force myself to smile and tell her how well I am feeling, in an effort to avoid that bizarre force-feeding.

I go out a bit, keeping up with the small, glamorous Hollywood clique. I bump into that cunning Warren Beatty again and he asks me humbly, cleverly: 'Do you remember me?'

'Just about . . .'

Resistance is futile with a man so overwhelmingly attractive – even more so in the flesh than on the screen. It could be fun to become Warren Beatty's obsession. I say goodbye and go on my way.

61

I'm drinking moderately, but I can't seem to stop the coke. I'm taking more than ever. Everyone takes it, including my doctor and lawyer. It was everywhere in those days.

I paint in a tutu. It is an eccentric, practical idea – I am always looking around for a cloth to wipe my hands, and can't stand those multicoloured drying-up cloths that make me feel as if I'm cooking, so I buy some flounced tulle tutus. It's entertaining to wipe myself down on them, and when there's no white left I just put on a new one.

This is a very creative time in my life. I splash great globs of colour onto the canvas and refine them with a brush, working away at the details, the shape of the eyes. I take my white pick-me-up, and paint night and day. One night I take too much and start hallucinating, my brain completely out of control.

Clint Eastwood has walked into my apartment dressed as a cowboy. He wants to kidnap me and seems determined. I hide in my room. I wait, I can hear his steps and all kinds of weird noises, I'm very afraid, and then it's silent again. Clint seems to have left. I wait for a while longer, my jaw and fists clenched, grinding my teeth and occasionally poking out my dehydrated tongue in a drug-induced grimace. I talk out loud to soothe myself, then inch open the door. I search every nook and cranny, trembling, and then get the hell out of there. I tear down the stairs and into the street, in my tutu. I knock at the first door I come to, a pretty, innocent-seeming house. A sweet young Frenchman opens. I tell him the whole story, in detail. He reassures me, tells me that I'm safe now. I ask him to call the police so they can come back to the apartment with me. He offers me a coffee and asks if I'm a dancer. I say yes. Where? I'm not sure right now, but if he's interested, I will remember tomorrow. He doesn't ask me any more questions. The police arrive, two officers whom I thank effusively and repeatedly. We go to my place. They search the apartment and don't find anything except ten grams of coke in full view on the bedside table; the dealer has just been round. They have my week's allowance – worth a small fortune – and their tone has become threatening.

'The choice is yours, Miss. Either flush this straight down the toilet or we'll be taking you to the station!'

I try to negotiate.

'You're not serious! Have some mercy, I've just escaped a kidnapping, surely you're not going to arrest me?!'

'Miss, get a grip on yourself. You have one minute.'

'Do you know how much that's worth? You want to share, is that it? OK! We'll go halves . . .'

One of the two becomes impatient and gets out his handcuffs. The effect is immediate; I let myself be escorted to the bathroom. As they leave they tell me, sweetly, that I have to give up this poison immediately; it's destroying half of Hollywood and can cause heart attacks.

I do stop using for a few days, but take it up again, unable to do without.

I paint, I dance to Donna Summer and I take care of my powder. Each time the doorbell rings unexpectedly I am terrified. I rush around the apartment stifling my shrieks, putting all the coke back in the bag, scraping down the coffee table, kitchen worktop, dressing table ... I stuff my drugs into a box of fortified cereal, turn the bath taps on full, inspect my nose, take off my tutu and eventually call out 'Coming!', all of a sudden languorous and slow-moving.

The police never came back, but I kept running.

I am snorting, running, collapsing and snorting again, more and more all the time. I no longer sleep. My face is shattered, hollow, my eyes bulging and mad. For the first time, I avoid looking at myself.

One night, blood flows out of my nose in two wide rivulets that run down into my mouth. I taste my own blood. It's very painful, and I am so afraid. I can't make the blood stop. I call for help and it comes quickly. At the hospital, compresses aren't enough to dry up the haemorrhage. I'm taken to the operating theatre, put under local anaesthetic and patched up. I'm returned to the ward, my nose deformed by a padded dressing. The doctor tells me that they've extracted a splinter of glass. It had been sucked up so strongly it perforated my nasal septum, already weakened by vasoconstriction. I learn of the fragility of this gristly inner wall, and of this common consequence of massive cocaine use. The septum cannot be completely repaired – I will always have a hole.

These days, weary of being told in medical examinations that my nasal septum is perforated, I avoid perfidious comment by giving them advance warning of the freak show: 'And now for the holey lady!'

My cocaine years were almost at an end. The addiction to illusion is strong, but the unstemmable blood, that taste of death and my panic all combined to reignite a will to live. I journey far into excess, never moderate, continuing until the final physical signs of self-destruction. But I always stop in time.

A session with my accountant straightened me out for good.

'OK, Sylvia, time to decide: it's the house or the coke!'

Being Dutch isn't all bad.

62

The telephone rings.

'Hello?'

'Hello, Sylvia, it's Warren Beatty.'

'Hello.'

'Do you remember me?'

Warren has retained that charming combination of candour and guile.

'Not really – you're an actor, is that right?!'

I make him laugh.

His voice is warm and soft, he must work on it, sharpening it as a powerful, slightly over the top seduction tool. When you hear him murmur 'it's Warren Beatty . . .', you immediately realise he's actually saying: 'Might the prospect of sleeping with me be agreeable to you?'

My response is not in the affirmative, and he is not used to that.

He wants to meet up with me, it's important, he finds me so attractive, so unusual, sensual, spiritual . . .

I agree, to cut short the list of compliments.

Warren is an influential man, not only an actor but a producer too, a big player, perfectly at home in the world of show business. Warren the Magnificent has seduced the whole of Hollywood; he could seduce a stone.

We arrange to meet at a luxury hotel. People warn me – apparently he always carries the key to a suite, just in case . . .

He does not come alone. He is accompanied by a silent 'assistant', who watches me and simpers as she moistens her lips. I'll later find out that he thought I liked women. The assistant was simply a pretty extra, that week's conquest.

We talk about cinema, projects, life in Los Angeles, art, literature. He is a refined, cultured man, much more impressive than your average Californian.

'Is it true that you've got a room key in your pocket?'

He laughs again. I really make him laugh, he says.

He changes the subject, asking me: 'What do you paint?'

'Naked women straddling enormous guns. I've just finished a canvas. It seems to be me, sitting astride a giant revolver.'

'Interesting . . . and symbolic?'

'Yes, of the dangers of sex, the perils of men!'

He laughs again.

I have to go. I claim a busy schedule when actually my afternoon is empty. This man is delightful, but I am feeling mischievous.

'Will I see you again?' he asks, as if his life depended on it.

'I'm sure. Hollywood is so tiny . . .'

I thank him for a pleasant time, take my leave of the lascivious, redundant assistant and scarper, walking tall.

'Stand tall! Hold your head high! It's not what's on the ground that's nigh!'

63

Menahem Golan and Yoram Globus are on the up and up.
They started the Cannon Group and are fast becoming very
influential.

'Some actors won't work with these "foreign peasants",'
Elaine tells me, 'but that's a big mistake . . .'

I get on well with these two men – slightly boorish for
sure, but warm-hearted, overflowing with genuine energy,
instinctive and ambitious yet respectful and even affectionate
when appropriate. Yoram has a fleeing eye, which I can't help
thinking must be a handicap in a business so dependent on
image, seduction and the ability to persuade. I immediately
advise him to have it fixed. He is surprised and a little disconcerted by my bluntness but follows my instructions and has
a successful operation a few months later. Yoram will become
one of the most powerful producers in the world – thanks to
me! We joke about this from time to time, Yoram not denying
the impact of my advice.

I will do a few films with Menahem and Yoram. This will be
a good thing. They will support me well over the years, staying
around even when my star declines. Menahem and Yoram will
offer me a rare and loyal affection and gratitude over a long
period of time.

64

'Hello, Sylvia, it's Warren Beatty!'

'Hello, Warren. I'm on.'

'On for what?'

'Our next meeting. At the same place, same time, tomorrow, alone. And I'm warning you, Sylvia is not Emmanuelle.'

I put the phone down.

I spent a wonderful few months under the spell of this gentle, funny and extraordinarily handsome man. I had the carefree feeling that our liaison would last no longer than a short season. He found me beautiful, different, a little crazy – just like his famous sister, as he used to say.

The conquest of women was for him an irrepressible urge, an endless hunting ground. It made me laugh to see him on the lookout like an animal – and just as overtly. He expressed his desire immediately, with great panache, and no woman had any cause to refuse this transient exchange, other than the frustration of becoming no more than a memory a few hours later. Warren had great powers of recall, and could describe in detail all the women he had loved since the start of his quest. I say 'loved' because Warren had the unique talent of being able to love for just a few hours – the love of an insect, short-lived and constantly renewed.

The obsessive predator did eventually calm down, but long after everyone else.

The lover is now a husband and father.

65

I'm going out tonight. I've been invited to a very famous film star's house for one of those Hollywood parties I usually don't attend, preferring to stay in my studio. But today I feel joyful and sociable, for no special reason. It's a good day.

I leave aside my Chanel suits, too dressy and thick for this permanent springtime, and slip into a silver lamé dress with a plunging neckline and back that I find hanging in my cupboard. Is it mine? A present? A costume? Left behind by someone else? It's the right size, and very close-fitting, meaning that I'll have to go naked under my party dress.

My white limousine drives through several security barriers without a problem. Stars keep themselves well protected; they have to, just a few miles from the dilapidated buildings of downtown LA, where whole forgotten sections of the city are a law unto themselves. My driver has forgotten the password for this inaccessible Malibu estate – a green concentrate of fertile soil, egocentric buildings and odd-shaped swimming pools, blue marks in the green millionaire's park dominating the hill and closed to the masses. I open the tinted window, smile, and offer my unknown name with confidence. Which is precisely the code. The armed guards are experienced, they can smell *star attitude* as Labradors sniff out drugs; they let me in.

The evening is billed as an appeal to generosity – funds will be raised for Amnesty International. Hollywood will drink to tortured prisoners, denouncing agony with its ecstasy.

The party is grand, shimmering. At the front gate I can already hear music and laughter. The lights on the lawn make my scales sparkle. There's a great density of film stars in this hilly garden, and the air is warm.

'Champagne?'

'Yes, please.'

My liver will forgive me. I flit around, smiling. You have to smile. I drink without greed, but without pause either. I dance. I've always loved to dance. Dancing has a therapeutic, hypnotic effect on me. The rhythm makes me move, empties me out and fills me with simple, physical pleasure.

Donna Summer again. I lift my arms, shimmy, toss my head around, sing a little loudly and spin in circles – a crazy silver spinning top. My dress extends my movements in small waves that die at my feet. I perform my show rarely these days, but always to the best of my ability. The beast is unleashed. My movements are supple, I brush against people, giving myself, intoxicated and light.

A well-dressed man applauds me, and introduces himself.

'Allan Turner.'

I smile. He is handsome, quite young, different, his hairstyle unusual. Its salt-and-pepper colour reassures me: he must be a man of experience.

'Two glasses, please!' he orders.

The man offers me his arm. I take it.

Three weeks later Allan Turner will ask for my hand in marriage. He's a businessman who has built a real-estate empire. He is rich, part of the jet set. In Los Angeles money makes you even more famous than glamour. Allan is wacky, too. He has an astonishing collection of red spectacles for someone so serious.

'Red goes with my hair! It's an important sign of difference in this homogeneous crowd!'

I have never been married, and am wearying of short-term love affairs. The request is delightful, spontaneous, perfect. You're on!

My mother is thrilled. Her lost, forsaken girl is getting married, returning at last to the straight and narrow.

The excesses of Las Vegas. It's a quickie marriage, with a small reception. We're staying at the very fashionable Caesar's Palace with the few guests and Allan's two daughters from his first marriage. I find the setting a little kitsch and tacky for such a commitment. I jump every time the room-service centurions enter our suite.

Allan isn't around much, all his time taken up once again by work. My honeymoon lasts just a few hours, and then I find myself alone, a sad young wife entertained only by the incessant comings and goings of the Roman soldiers. I call my mother in tears; she has remained in Europe.

'Never mind!' she says.

The straight and narrow is a dead end.

After six months Allan confesses, just as sweetly as he had asked for my hand, that he has made a mistake and would like to get divorced. I am given time to think.

Arthur has come over for a short holiday. Allan is an

impatient character who doesn't like sharing what still belongs to him. He files for divorce.

The law allows me to demand half of Allan's fortune. This seems disproportionate to the amount of time we spent together.

I accept what he wants to give me, and go.

Elaine is upset.

'But my poor darling, you'll never be rich! Marriage is a business like any other!'

No, not everything is business. I married not as an investment but out of hope. I will not be rich, but my conscience will be clear, and on my deathbed the linen will be fine and peace will shine from my lips in a final, candid, eternal smile.

66

The young woman is pretty, but not overly so. Everything about her is impeccable. Every time she moves something shines – silk, a diamond, lacquer – the image is constantly twinkling. The young woman is talking with suppressed ardour to an equally impeccable and gleaming man. He is the lover. The heroine has been given a nice American name with a touch of exoticism to make it different. Usually her first name will end in *a*. The setting is plush and comfortable, and the hair styled and sprayed. Material life may be completely under control but the heart is eternally hurting, and Scotch is drunk at any time without producing the slightest effect. When love is born and seems to last in this near-perfect paradise, a prettier woman will inevitably appear, or a shattering piece of news, to render impossible this union that everyone, including me, has been so thrilled about. Everything is ruined by an unsuspected infidelity or an appalling family secret that the grandmother reveals sitting next to an artificial fireplace, her smooth face set off by a big pearl necklace. Jonathan is in fact the half-brother of Cynthia – their mother was generous with her favours. Cynthia collapses in the arms of her contrite mother. She loses her prince but finds a longed-for brother. Emotions are at their peak. The dream is crushed by dreadful reality, but hope remains immortal. The fiery princess lying dormant in Cynthia will always get the better of fate's cruel blows, she swears it, weeping, and Granny has the final word in the provisional ending. She claims, from experience, that living is forgiving and that love will be reborn. I hope so too. Yes, in the next episode Cynthia will be happy.

After my divorce I discovered a soft, sweet drug, a potent antidepressant vital to my state of mind: soap operas. These deliciously light and repetitive programmes have helped me to sleep and have woken me up almost every day for the last twenty years. I am addicted to their sunset promises, and to the stylish, complex lives that keep me waiting breathless for the next instalment. The people around me laugh; I do too but I keep on watching.

So here I am, alone again, totally alone in this vast Los Angeles, talking to my paintings.

I am painting more and more, huge canvases, bright colours, always of beautiful young women.

I fly to Europe for a new film.

67

My feet are naked in the grass, bleached by the frost. I accept this suffering without a word, as if I deserved it. My hair is long, wavy and wet. I am cold, and running away. The day has dawned diffuse and everything is covered in thick fog. How can I find my bearings in this sunless English countryside? The dawn is gloomy and I hate these owl screeches, they make me jump.

I have returned to working with Just Jaeckin, as his Lady Chatterley. The scene is unusually powerful. I have to shout while running, what a challenge!

My lines are full of hysteria: 'I'm obsessed! I'm obsessed!'

Finding these words in myself soothes my rage and gives me new energy. I delight in the thought of disturbing this rustic calm, this hypocritical harmony.

I am obsessed ... obsessed with the love that eludes me. A modern fable, the curse of the naked woman.

The start of the *Lady Chatterley's Lover* shoot is depressing. I arrive from Los Angeles, where English drizzle exists only as an artificial spray, to find the sky lower each morning than it was the day before. The fog remains on the ground for hours. I am empty and restless. I'm working.

*

'Champagne!'

'No, darling, tea!'

Elaine has come with me. She knows that I am fragile, even more so than usual, and is taking care of me. She comes to collect me every morning at 6 a.m. – the middle of my night. She wakes me with affectionate, bracing, amusing words. 'Hi, honey! Hello, darling! Come on! Up! Don't be lazy. The sun is not shining this morning, as it didn't yesterday, or the day before . . . who cares? Me!'

My Russian doll follows me everywhere, so strong and calm. Elaine knits as a way through boredom, for hours at a time, regularly raising her eyes from the sweater to watch over me. Elaine's creations keep me warm, and she also buys me a tartan car rug made out of lambswool that she spotted in the village.

'Lovely colours, don't you think?'

Elaine is never short of ideas. She has decided to put me on tea therapy. Litres of honeyed tea that she hands me with love and that I drink for her sake alone.

'Well done, darling!'

The words of a mother.

Caffeine abuse and frozen feet bring me back to life.

I notice a prince charming, producer André Djaoui, whose name amuses me: 'Nice to see you, Mr Vowels!'

André is tall, refined and stimulating. He impresses me, and picks me up. I live this bond like it's the last. I hope. I think this union can endure, I believe in love with him. A lovely shoot punctuated by wonderful, deep, romantic trysts with André.

On the last day of filming I decide to cut my hair. The long locks fall to the floor as I spur on my stylist.

'Nice and short, please!'

She swears that everything suits me. We shall see. Goodbye, Lady Chatterley and your princess curls. I throw out my costume. I want to mark the end of the fiction, to experience love for real.

André hates the woman I have become. Even though it's only hair, I have broken the spell. He drops me from his life once the film is over, as is normal in this world. Each break-up hurts me more than the last. I love André much more than he loves me. I can't bear goodbyes these days. Telling each other over a coffee that you don't love each other any more, won't be seeing each other any more ... all these 'no mores' are unbearable to me. Why, when there's no reason for it? The split does me a lot of harm. I need continuity, a thread. Does love really die? I prefer the idea that the people I have loved are still at my side, never far away, appearing sometimes in dreams, responding sweetly when I call. Why split up? Why put this irreversible end to a diminished love? I love you less, my heart no longer beats faster when I see you, but I still love you; so let's see each other less, but still see each other.

Exit Sylvia. He no longer loves me, never did love me. It's absurd. I am a trophy, a 'must fuck'. Make love with Emmanuelle the pleasure queen, then return home. Take her, drunken and dazed, barely consenting. Come and then leave.

68

At that time of my life I was searching for love, wishing for it, dreaming of it. I was weary of myself. I was starting to see my solitude stretching out before me as if decreed by fate. I needed another, a bond, I was bored of playing around. But also somehow convinced that the love of the public – that generous fervour I had longed for – was incompatible with the love of one man. A single man would explode under the massive impact of the public's love. I realised helplessly how the ravages of desire prevail over love. Am I merely desirable, doomed only to intense, short-lived desire?

Can one die of a failure to find love?

Not me. If I die, it will be of a real, not a virtual pain.

To die of love ... what a lovely end, though – the height of romanticism. What a girl I am!

I am reminded of Betty. It was at the hotel, before boarding school – I must have been ten years old. I can still remember the woman's face, and her arm ...

Betty arrives one spring day, with her lovely smile.

'She must be at least forty,' says my aunt Alice, who is always pondering other people's ages. Aunt Alice likes to guess at the passing of time on people's faces, and assures me that she is rarely mistaken.

Betty is of average height, with average-length hair – everything about her seems average. Her hair is dark, her skin clear, she has a lovely, almost constant smile which makes her eyes seem moist with unshed tears. She wears a warm, fine-knit cream suit and a long brown silk scarf patterned with multi-coloured hearts.

'It's my lucky charm!' she cries, straightening the scarf on her shoulder.

'How long will you be staying at the hotel?' asks my aunt.

'I'm not sure, long enough . . .'

'Long enough?'

'Yes, long enough that I leave happy.'

Betty takes her key, refusing my aunt's offer to help carry her two heavy suitcases. Aunt Alice is pleased; the more luggage, the longer the stay.

She gives Betty the best room, with a bath and a backlit dressing table in which she can gaze at herself and doll herself up.

'Strange, isn't she? Don't you think?'

I don't reply. I like her even though I don't know her. She seems to be waiting, but what for?

A few days later Aunt Alice rushes towards me, pointing at an advert in the newspaper.

'Look, it's her!'

She reads in a low voice – Aunt Alice always spoke quietly: '"Pleasant young woman, good job, likes poetry, travel and flowers, seeks mature man for serious relationship. Send your letters to Betty Ulmer, Commerce Hotel, Station Square, Utrecht."'

Mary (the exuberant aunt) grabs the advert and shouts:

'Young woman! Hardly. It will never work. Without an exact age men will think it's a con, and anyway, flowers and travel are expensive. She should have mentioned cooking and sewing, not poetry.'

Aunt Mary reads the advert several times, smiling at such naivety. Aunt Alice takes back the newspaper and says: 'If she's planning to stay here until she gets married, that's great for us ...'

'Any post for me?' asks Betty.

'No, ma'am, I'm afraid not. Perhaps tomorrow.'

'Yes, of course, it must take a little while. Have a nice day – I'm off to the flower market!'

'Any post today?'

'No, Betty – tomorrow, I'm sure.'

Aunt Alice's voice is doubtful.

Betty strokes her soft silk scarf and walks out of the hotel. She has been here almost a month, without a single reply to her adverts. All she's received are a few letters from her concerned mother. Sometimes she waves at me from her bedroom, having left the door open, and asks me in. She has stuck up her travel photos, as well as photos of her father and her 'handsome Italian' with the toothy smile – a previous lover, she says. She has carried a child in her belly, which she hid and then lost. I am stunned by this new version, I can't understand it. No cabbage patch, no birds and bees – a child in the belly? My aunt is right, Betty is a bit strange. She's a teacher who's taken indeterminate leave in order to find love. She likes tulips, especially the marquise ones with their velvety purple pointed petals. Betty has three regrets: her lost child, love not yet known, and the fact that tulips have no scent. When drunk on brandy she says that in fact she is sure tulips do have a scent, it's just imperceptible to humans.

'A little like me,' she whispers in my ear, but I don't understand.

This morning the hotel is woken by Aunt Alice's loud, shrill screams. Betty has hanged herself. My aunt discovered her on the floor, the ripped-out chandelier next to her head and her lucky-charm scarf wrapped tight around her neck.

Through my half-open door I see the stretcher in the hallway, with a white sheet over Betty and her arm hanging out – long, limp and dead. Betty offering her hand as she leaves.

I remember Aunt Alice's sadness when a few days later she threw out two envelopes addressed to Betty.

'The post is so slow . . .' she murmured.

One of the letters had a pretty heart on the back. I picked it out of the rubbish and read it aloud to Betty that evening, leaning out of my window looking up to heaven, stumbling over words I didn't understand.

69

A journalist asks about my political views at a press conference to promote *Lady Chatterley's Lover*. This is unexpected, and flattering. I don't reply, in order to stay within the framework of prepared responses, but I do request a private interview. Raghid is a freelance journalist, an adventurer. He reminds me of André. André was a Moroccan Jew and Raghid is Muslim but they share that life-affirming complexion, and the warmth, gentle virility, honeyed voice and feeling for the sensual life. Raghid is attractive, self-confident, independent. He seems perfect, and completely under my spell. I could do whatever I wanted with him, but I am weary.

Raghid woos me in dazzling, princely fashion but I do not respond. He persists; it's a cultural thing, he says in his defence. I remain deaf to his advances. I receive forty magnificent red roses on an almost daily basis. I keep them, unable to throw away flowers. The doorbell rings.

'Your roses, Miss Kristel . . .'

My bed is covered in superb gifts that I send back. They hold no meaning but I keep the flowers as any woman would, wait for them even, becoming dependent on them but still thinking myself free.

One morning Raghid's roses seem to have a sweeter, more

subtle fragrance than they did before. I surrender, saying yes to this Arab prince. Let him whisk me away!

Return to Los Angeles. I am surprised by Raghid the journalist's lifestyle. He belongs to the Lebanese upper class, and is related to the Saudi royal family.

I thought I was well acquainted with luxury, but through Raghid I discover the most opulent lifestyle this world can provide, a hidden elite living in palaces with golden door-knobs, flying the world in private jets – not those small planes with the tiny engines, but real Boeings with lounges, beds, jacuzzis, film screens and great globs of grey caviar.

Raghid's relations are Arab princes who travel the world for a horse race, an opera or a fashion show, or to gamble huge sums in Las Vegas and Monte Carlo. I sometimes go along – a fashionable, chaperoned icon.

Raghid idolises me, and this adoration makes me nervous. He tells me he would be most honoured if I would convert to Islam and become his wife. I ask, with great courtesy, for some time to think.

What would this entail? I'd have to learn the Koran and apply its rules. I'd be entering a modern form of Islam, that of the Gucci- and Valentino-clad women I meet. My self-expression would be constrained and my film career limited or stopped. Raghid would provide for my every need and we would start a big family. The word 'family' still has a stimulating effect on me, I am always tempted to cry: oh yes, a family, a real family, let's do it now! But that's impossible, and the rest of the pro-gramme is less appealing. Alcohol – which I am still allowed in my role as Western film star – would soon be prohibited to me.

Converting would be sure to make two people extremely upset: my mother and Sister Marie Immaculata.

Raghid says he's more in love than he has ever been. Is this true, or simply the ephemeral expression of his exuberant personality? Will he in a few months tell me that he was mistaken? He leaves messages on the fridge for me: 'Read the Koran!', 'Don't drink!', 'Learn belly dancing!'

I am looking for love but I want to keep the only thing I have left – a bit of freedom. I decline Raghid's offer, with a level of diplomacy I didn't know I had. He is hurt and angry and opposes my refusal. This stubbornness frightens me.

We attend a New Year's Eve dinner at a Paris nightclub. All Raghid's friends are there, from all around the world. I wear a more revealing dress than usual; it clings to my body, it gleams. Under Raghid's disapproving gaze I regularly ask for fresh supplies of champagne. My voice and laughter become louder; I flirt with my neighbours, even going so far as to brush a few cheeks with my hands. At dessert I excuse myself and head for the dance floor. My hips roll as I dance. I notice Raghid's driver a little way off in the corner, shuffling timidly. I walk towards him, hold out my hand and ask him to dance. We dance. Raghid, who normally stays very sober, has had a few drinks. He charges onto the dance floor and drags me away. We meet for a cognac the next day, at the Café Deux Magots. I am dismissed, freed by mutual agreement. He sends me back to Amsterdam in a white Rolls-Royce, with a final bouquet on the back seat.

I go home to Los Angeles. I intend to paint a little more in the California sun before returning to my own country. I am tired of Hollywood. I've had enough of the spectacle of these creatures desperate to resemble each other, these vitamin-enriched clones lifting weights on Venice Beach, jogging, or else stuffing themselves with sugar and fat the moment they aren't working. The old must die wrinkle-free, hands spotted but nails immaculate, exhausted from smiling as a profession, burnt out by their stampede for riches.

70

In 1982 I organise my first exhibition, in Los Angeles. It's a success. I am complimented by art-world professionals who don't know who I am. My canvases sell well. I react shyly, filled with wonder and doubt at hearing the word 'talent' applied to me.

Lady Chatterley's Lover marked an important point in my career. It was my last successful movie. The rest would be rough, unseen, done for the money.

I still find the end of a shoot just as brutal. The end of Curtis Harrington's *Mata Hari*, in 1984, is a horrible memory – the first black hole. I was in love and it was over. I had thought and hoped the affair would carry on, but I was wrong. We were shooting in Budapest. We were a happy, domesticated couple. We went to an Elton John concert. I listened to those songs – the loveliest of which are infinitely sad – as a light, warm rain drenched my dress. I was melting, he was caressing me and holding my hand, I was experiencing an isolated moment of perfect grace. My lover was married but never mentioned it. I hoped. This tenderness deserved to continue.

The film came to an end, and he left. As usual. Film people seem to embrace this rhythm of short-term, nomadic loves. I can't get used to it, I hope too much. I count on the love lasting, but it isn't even there – there is no love in the movies. Just frenzy and ego-rubbing; a game for empty, damaged, fragile but hardened creatures. The actor never stops acting.

My lover flew away. He lives in another country. We said goodbye in an airport corridor. I didn't cry, I was drunk – a hangover was my first withdrawal symptom. I swapped champagne definitively for hard liquor. Opting for quick oblivion, for the speedy destruction of all this drama.

I continue to live off my name, a first name – my only role – Emmanuelle.

In this use of me there is a mistake, an abuse, a total and violent conflict with who I am. I may smile, may act carefree and consenting, may continue speaking up for sexual freedom and asserting that in Nordic countries nudity is considered normal. But none of this erotic universe is in the least bit natural to me. I draw on inspiration, on my imagination, on other people's desire, but not on my own experience. I continue being cast against type, telling myself that I have no choice.

In 1984 I make an appearance in Francis Leroi's *Emmanuelle 4*, passing the baton to Mia Nygren, a very young and beautiful model.

Years later I will appear in some soft-core American TV serials on the theme of *Emmanuelle*. All I do is sit quietly on an aeroplane next to my fictive husband – George Lazenby, a former James Bond – and remember with him the licentious times past. The flashback sex scenes are played by other Emmanuelles. The vein seems inexhaustible, and I'm not the only one to exploit it – poor Emmanuelle has seen everything. *Black Emmanuelle* makes an appearance, then a whole string of preposterous titles: *Emmanuelle in Space, Emmanuelle and the Nuns, Emmanuelle and the Vampires* ...

My favourite is the silliest: *Emmanuelle and the Last Cannibals* ... good thing I escaped!

71

My mother is slumped in front of the TV, chain-smoking. The smoke coils out of her tired, half-open mouth. She drinks a little, sipping sweet, warm sherry. My mother will watch television in precisely this way, every night for the rest of her life. She always crashes out here, her palm opening and relinquishing the tiny glass at last, her limp arm unfolding, a grey snow spreading across the screen. Arthur is ten years old, asleep in his room. He often gets up in the middle of the night and pads into the smoky living room in which everything that was once white – the net curtains, the embroidered cotton tablecloth, my mother's teeth – has been yellowed by tobacco. He picks up the glass, empties the ashtray, shakes his grandmother's arm with childish affection and says to her: 'You're sleeping, Granny, you'd be more comfortable in your bed . . .'

Tonight my mother stays awake longer than usual, she's in a good mood. She dreams – awake – of happy things that make her smile. My mother is roaming and dancing in her dreams, full of hope. The sun must have been out today. She will sleep well, in the living room.

It's morning. My mother wakes, drinks her coffee and smokes, before breakfast.

The doorbell rings. It's very early.

She leaps up, pats her flattened hair, moves towards the door and shouts: 'Who is it?'

No response.

Ring! Ring!

'Who is it, for heaven's sake?'

No reply. The door isn't locked and the knob turns from the outside. My mother backs away silently. The door opens wide and fast on an unknown man, in a hurry, his face obscured by a motorbike helmet. My mother is in danger, and brandishes her burning cigarette like a weapon.

'Stop that! It's me! It's me . . .'

My father steps into the apartment, puts his helmet on the floor and holds out his arms to my mother.

'Aren't you going to kiss me?'

My mother can't get a single word out. And yet she is not surprised, she knew he would come back, sooner or later, how could it be otherwise? The only thing she didn't know was when. So it's today. Some bonds are stronger than us; the story is unfinished, and will perhaps have no end. You don't decide to stop love. My father has come back.

'Well, say something!'

'Hello . . .'

My mother is trembling slightly. She would like to have been able to prepare herself a little, to doll herself up, to not display so clearly that she has spent this time killing it, waiting. Dependency is not attractive. And this is such an ugly setting for a moment like this. The solid layer of tobacco smoke on the living-room walls is suddenly unbearable to my mother. If she could she would have cleaned each piece of furniture, polished the wooden floor, bleached the tablecloth and made this place a welcoming, gleaming haven. My father has come back.

'Would you like something to drink, a coffee, a –'

'A cognac, please!'

'Of course! What am I thinking? I must have some ...'

My father sits down, drinks, takes my mother's hand. He wants to talk to her. He wants to say how often he has thought of her, all these years, and how much he regrets the pain he has caused her. He couldn't help that sudden, forced ending. He was physically dependent. He has come in secret, he doesn't know how long he will be able to stay before the other woman comes to find him – because she is still around, alive and kicking. And if she comes, he will go back. His life is there now. The damage has been done, but he wanted my mother to know that she is still in his heart. He reminds her of that first ball, of the way they couldn't stop looking at each other. My mother listens and says nothing. She leaves her hand in my father's hand. She drinks with him and starts counting the passing time once more. How much longer will my father stay?

One week. My father stayed one week. A few days of happiness, conversation, chaste and loving gestures. My father played football with Arthur, slept in my mother's bed. They got up late, drank, shouted and laughed, and didn't cry.

Hanny came for my father. She parked next to his motor-bike. She didn't get out, just beeped as you whistle for a dog. The sports car revved several times, and my father came out. He followed her on his motorbike. He left. My mother wasn't sad – on the contrary. She was relieved, liberated, reassured by this final gesture, this proof.

She carried on waiting.

72

I miss my son. Terribly. I never express this, because I know there is no alternative. Nothing about my job, or state, allows me to look after my son like a mother on an ongoing basis. In my sporadic moments of lucidity Arthur's absence is like a heavy weight, pressing down on my guts, twisting them. I talk aloud to him, tell him I'm thinking of him, that I'll make up for lost time. That my filming and painting is for us, for him, that in fact I am him. I will try to find the solidity to come back, to collect him and never leave him again. At the end of these resounding monologues I wait in silence, with no reply. No child's laughter, no mispronounced words. Then, after a moment, I sense something in the air, whistling through the open bay window, a breeze of imaginary forgiveness that brushes my skin and soothes me. I dream of my son waiting quietly for me.

73

Elaine has a meeting with an aspiring director, a certain Philippe Blot, in which he presents her with a script so absurd she tears it up. Its title is *The Arrogant*.

'But,' he cries, 'only Sylvia Kristel can play this part!'

The man insists, charming Elaine into giving him my contact details in Amsterdam, where I am on holiday. The man turns up two days later with a pair of lively assistants. He is French, extremely likeable and considerate. We get on well. He is a paparazzo and wants me to help with his redeployment. That makes me laugh! He flatters me, I smile at this delightful man with the muscular body; he seems like a strong person. He leaves me with a copy of *The Arrogant*, begging sweetly for my attention. 'At least read the beginning . . .'

'You must have a lot of time on your hands!' says Elaine on the phone.

'But he's so charming . . .'

I am a little lost. My status has dropped, my forties are looming. This paparazzo is full of ideas and drive, and he's offering me a project. He has crossed the seas for me, he is dynamic and charming, and I am bored and alone. The rest of the story is logged in newspaper articles, lawyers' files and the mists of my memory.

I marry Philippe, vaguely in love. We make three films

together, the unforgettable *Arrogant* in 1987, *In the Shadow of the Sandcastle* in 1990, and *Hot Blood* in 1991. Three films generously produced by Menahem and Yoram. Three third-rate flops.

I can remember the plot of *The Arrogant,* more or less:

A biker is fleeing his brothers-in-law on his powerful machine. He has killed their father and fucked their wives. The crassness of that term is fitting. These men are therefore determined to find the criminal, nicknamed the Arrogant because he thinks he is God's gift to women. On the road he picks up a hitch-hiker, a dropout waitress on her way to work. That's me. They enliven their flight by sleeping together. Still on the road, the fleeing couple meet another couple with whom they of course decide to fuck, in many different positions. This slows them down and the brothers-in-law, drunk on revenge, start to catch up. At the end the Arrogant is thought to be dead, but reappears. I too have survived, and go wearily back to work . . .

There are many similarities between this film and my life with Philippe.

Philippe was not exactly a criminal, but he was an extremely self-confident seducer, megalomaniac and smooth talker, as Elaine had said. We were constantly on the run. No avenging brothers-in-law but plenty of seduced investors looking to collect massive debts.

Philippe watches over me, keeping an eye on the physical state of the hen expected to lay his golden eggs. He looks after me as a circus trainer takes care of his beast, monitoring my food and forbidding me to drink in the run-up to the shoots and business meetings he arranges. To ensure my necessary and sporadic sobriety he has me prescribed Antabuse, a powerful pill which when mixed with alcohol provokes violent palpitations, immediate headaches and sometimes vomiting.

Then, if the beast has been docile and performed well, he allows it to drink again. He takes me out for dinner and a 'nice bottle of wine'! I'm allowed alcohol just as I become too sober, too lucid.

Philippe is very sweet with children. He has two sons who are often around, and he treats Arthur with genuine affection. He would like us to enlarge our family, but that isn't possible.

I want to see my forgotten father again. I haven't seen him for an eternity, not since the court case. My brother visits him from time to time, and gives me snatches of news; this time he has warned me that our father's health is in serious decline. I have sensed, even from far away, that I need to see him again.

Philippe comes with me.

My father opens the door without a word; he hasn't recognised me.

'Hello. It's Sylvia.'

I am shocked by the state of my father – thin, white-haired, bearded, a bit like a tramp. Hanny is still there, aloof; she'd rather we didn't come in so suggests we go for a walk. I say I'm not well, in a bid to have some time alone with my father. She goes with Philippe. My father still isn't saying anything. I'm looking for the flamboyant man, the artist.

'Pour me a beer, Daddy?'

We drink beer together, with Jenever chasers. My father opens his heart. He says he has changed. He has indeed, so much that my head is spinning with feelings. He is quite lucid, and apologises for not having recognised me. He didn't think he would ever see me again, it's been more than ten years. I feel weak. I never thought my father could age this much. I have had that childish conviction that there was still time, that I could finish my journey, my solitary education, and then come back to him. Time has passed, and there isn't much left. I am horrified by all these years I can see in my father's face. I must come to terms with the fact that he will die, with this feeling of incompleteness. We won't have time. I pull myself together. He's still speaking:

'You know, my life is wretched. We're always arguing but I no longer have the strength. Your mother was different, conciliatory.'

I don't say anything. He carries on, recovering with the alcohol a little of his arrogance.

'Is your son well? What's his name again? Do you find time to look after him? I haven't been a good father.'

I tell him that that is far in the past, now, and then tell him again how hurt I was by the lies of the tabloid press. He in turn tells me that he has forgotten.

Philippe and Hanny come back.

The visit is over.

I hug my father for the last time. I know it.

He died a few weeks later, from a stroke. It made the local newspaper. I only heard days after his death, through my sister. I was in Los Angeles, it was too late to get to the funeral. His wife didn't want me there, in any case. I had flowers sent, I prayed and cried.

His wife lived on for a long time. Virulent diabetes led to the amputation of one leg, and then the other. Even as a cripple she found a replacement for my father without much trouble. She's dead now.

74

Philippe never had any money, which was a real problem because he spent a great deal. I occasionally emerged sufficiently from my fog to worry about our situation, alerted by certain registered-post letters that had escaped Philippe's watchful eye and that I happened to come across. He invariably replied: 'Everything is going fine, sweetheart. Everything is fine!'

I have kept from that time a tendency to panic whenever someone tells me that 'everything is fine'.

In fact, nothing was fine.

We leave Los Angeles for Paris, and then for St-Tropez where we live in a magnificent Provençal house a moment from the sea on Boulevard Patch, miraculously bought on credit. We employ a secretary, a chef and a personal trainer. I occasionally find official notices stuck to the door. The bailiffs come by more and more often. Philippe invites them in for champagne, and then they leave. His response is always the same: 'Everything is fine, sweetheart!'

Philippe's mother often comes to stay, and I express my surprise at her calm amid all these bailiffs. She pulls a small pack of tranquillisers out of her handbag.

'Here's my secret. Xanax.'

I apply the formula, and sink a little deeper into my fog.

I now leave my room only to take my dog Danone out for great long walks along the beach, once the busyness of summer is over. I am lethargic, depressed for the first time in my life, washed up.

Then one day there's a yellow cordon – a seizure authorisation – encircling the house and gate.

. Philippe tells me that we have to leave. I follow him. I leave it all behind, hoping to come back soon: my devoted dog, my canvases, a few valuable works of art bought from around the world, my princess dresses, my jewellery, photos of my son and family. Everything. We flee hastily to Los Angeles with a couple of suitcases.

Philippe immediately rents a superb house and a sports car. I question this luxury. He says: 'Appearances are the important thing; people believe whatever you show them . . .'

A close friend of Hugo's called Freddy De Vree comes to visit. I confide my weariness, my fears, this flight whose end I cannot imagine. He sweetly offers me his hospitality should I ever decide to return to Europe, and leaves me his phone number in Brussels.

Philippe and I are once again on the run – to Madrid this time.

Philippe arranges a meeting with a new bank, and tells me to go to Chanel to buy something nice to wear.

I refuse. I ask for detailed explanations, dispense with the alcohol and medications for a few days and demand facts, figures, dates. I won't take one more step without a proper explanation.

Philippe reminds me that we were guarantors together for a

film that was never made. He brandishes a document that does indeed bear my signature. We have spent the money and the financiers want to be repaid, which is why we are on the run. I would never have suspected something so serious, such a massive debt . . . I had just trusted, slept, kept my eyes shut.

I express my fear of going to prison, and my shame. I tell him that I come from a family with respect for money, that all this hurts me, is unbearable, has got to stop. Philippe forbids me to leave and tells me I have no choice: we are still married, bound together. I call my old friend Wim Verstappen. I talk to him in Dutch, which Philippe doesn't understand, and ask him to send me a plane ticket. I cite a necessary visit to my son, and my mother's poor state of health.

I leave, and don't come back.

75

Leaving Philippe didn't pay off my debts. I discover the real extent of the damage once I'm single. I have earned a lot of money in my life; in the 1970s, my fee per film could be as much as $300,000. An apartment in LA, houses in Holland, Paris and Ramatuelle on the French Riviera. I have nothing left. When I ask for a few family photos to be returned, they write that this will be impossible because my personal souvenirs may have a market value that will contribute to paying off the debt. I have lost everything, but not everything has been repaid. A debt incurred by a privately agreed loan in 1989 levied against me an army of bailiffs that pursued me for years.

I try to defend myself, to describe how that signature took place in a fog, how I would have signed anything when I was either drunk or desperate to be left in peace. In vain. I am responsible, the debt must be paid in full. The Monagasque investors remain deaf to my pleas. They are precise, quibbling, determined and humiliating. They lie in wait for any income, keeping themselves informed, watching the newspapers and then knocking at any door whenever and wherever they please.

On the eve of a private view in Antwerp – more than ten years after the first proceedings – the bailiffs told me that I would not be able to sell the canvases I was about to exhibit. Several years' worth of work impounded.

Philippe carried on regardless. One of his girlfriends contacted me recently; she explained that she had lost a lot of money, and asked me to pursue him with her. I refused. No revenge – I leave men to their own consciences.

Wim welcomes me warmly to his house in Amsterdam.

I am nearly forty years old. Strangely, my body is still in good shape. It must be genetic. My body is going strong but I myself am packing up. Being on the run has worn me out. I had hidden before, but never fled. I am very vulnerable, and ask Freddy De Vree for help.

He comes to find me straight away. Freddy is spontaneous, unpredictable, generous. He is a journalist, an expert on modern art and a poet.

Freddy takes care of me like a loving nurse, with a thoughtfulness I have never known. He tells me clearly that he doesn't want me to drink. This is non-negotiable. If I drink, I leave. He doesn't want any drama, any chaos. He is authoritative, and I carry out his orders. To give myself a hand and to remain worthy of his trust, I take Antabuse. We drink non-alcoholic beer, and one evening I comment to Freddy that it tastes so good one would never know. Then suddenly I start shaking violently, having cheerfully downed two glasses. I am sweating, I can't breathe. This non-alcoholic beer is in fact the normal kind. The waiter has made a mistake.

I stop drinking for several years.

Freddy can't stand laziness. I follow his strict, kindly regime of compulsory activities: light home cooking, lymphatic drainage, long walks, love, and ten drawings a day.

'Why ten?' I ask.

'Because of those ten, one will be great, two will be good, and you can throw out the rest.'

My movie career has slowed right down, which is a good thing; I am becoming a painter. My new French agent, Monita, finds me cameo roles and a few paid TV appearances, just enough to live on without attracting the attention of the bailiffs.

I am invited to Marseilles to sit on the jury of a film festival. I still love the movies. I accept.

The organisers seem disappointed to see me so shabbily dressed and un-dolled up. They were expecting a little more glamour and gloss. I left my last real designer dresses in the St-Tropez wardrobes, swearing to myself as I left that I would never again buy beautiful clothes, or jewellery – nothing that could be seized, that could remind me of this. Luckily there are a few ambitious young actresses on the jury, decked out in sexy clothes.

I overhear them in the toilets as I stand motionless and out of sight in a cubicle:

'What the fuck is Emmanuelle doing here?! She's not even an actress . . .'

I don't say anything, I don't dare. I'm not used to this. I'd naively thought that inviting me must have meant they appreciated me at least a little. I emerge from the cubicle only once I'm sure the young actresses have well and truly left. I flee Marseilles, flee France: no more drama!

76

My life with Freddy is harmonious. This man is my final refuge, and I know it. I leave him sometimes, and come back. I am faithful. I safeguard his freedom, and my own – the space needed to create. When I want to experience life elsewhere, I go off for a few days, taking advantage of these infrequent escapades to allow myself what is forbidden to me: drink.

I go off by myself in spite of my reluctance to travel alone. My atrophied sense of direction is a legacy from being a star, from that perpetually guided existence. To compensate, I take every precaution to make my trip as smooth as possible. I pack my suitcase meticulously – everything is wrapped, sorted, folded. I get hold of contact details for people and organisations that may be useful in the foreign land, and arrive at the train station or airport many hours early. Despite all these precautions designed to limit the unexpected, my solitary trips usually turn into some kind of adventure.

I am returning from Amsterdam, from a poignant visit to my mother who loses a little more of her vitality each time I see her. On the train I close my eyes and images flood my mind – the hotel (now razed to the ground), my industrious, silent, beautiful mother sewing my dresses . . .

I find the bar carriage. I want to drive away these dark

thoughts with a nice cold beer, then several. We're approaching Brussels and I am realising how drunk I am. A smiling young man sitting opposite recognises me and asks me pleasantly to sign an autograph, which I do with gusto. We start an intimate conversation. He is studying film. He flatters me, buys me more beers, then tells me how sad he is that we'll have to say goodbye in a few moments.

'Don't be sad, I'll get off with you!'

I can't kiss Freddy in this state. It would hurt him, he would think that all his efforts and love had been in vain. He would think I was sick, he would lecture me. I can't go home.

'Perfect, come to my place!'

'Fine.'

We smoke an enormous joint, and I wake up fully dressed in a double bed next to the sleeping young man, shocked to see a dog tearing my passport to pieces. I get up in silent fury, salvage part of my identity and return to Brussels.

77

Freddy has decided to overcome my 'frigidity'. What he calls frigidity is in fact a mixture of weariness and tenacious modesty. He invents erotic games that make me even less responsive. I don't say anything, I don't want to hurt him. He trains me to walk around the flat naked, and does it himself too – I can't help laughing at this home nudist camp.

78

My father's death extinguished my mother. It's as simple as that. She lost her enthusiasm, her desires, her smile; each day she was a little slower, more silent, moved a little less.

My mother was waiting for my father. He had come back once; he would do so again. Little by little she started to lose her memory. She forgot out of indifference and because she wanted to, eliminating everything that didn't have to do with my father. She seemed to be endlessly looking for him. She would go off in the car for hours at a time, coming back shattered and unable to say where she had been. This went on for quite a few years, my mother wild, lonely, in love and wandering.

Then she started forgetting more and more things: to close the door or switch off the lights, people's names ... She distanced herself from her daily life, from her unbearable routine.

Senile dementia was diagnosed, and my mother was put permanently into a nursing home. At particularly bad moments she would often speak in English, saying 'We are from Utrecht!' or 'My daughter is a big star, you know!' or 'I'm sorry, the hotel is full.'

She was moved several times. As soon as she was starting to recognise her bedroom, to find her way and remember a few faces, the department of public health would decide to move her. I asked the reason for all this moving, so upsetting to my mother. There was no reason. I was furious. These changes seemed done on purpose – an integral part of a strategy to accelerate the death of useless, senile people. After a few hours she would understand that she was in a new place, grumble a bit and then fall silent. One day she slipped over and was left paralysed down one side and unable to speak clearly. She stopped feeding herself. She spat everything out, rejecting it. She wanted to die, she said so.

We came to see her one last time, the whole family reunited around my mother. The nurse said to us: 'As long as you're here she'll stay alive; she's been waiting for you.'

My mother could still say my name, moving her weakened mouth with excruciating slowness. She looked at me tenderly, moving her dry, sticky tongue in and out. I wet a flannel and wrung it, drip by drip, into my mother's mouth as she moaned and turned her head.

We all kissed my mother on the forehead.

I kept my lips on her for a long time, the time of a thank-you, the infinite time of all the unsaid love I was depositing on her. We left.

They strapped a piece of cloth around my mother's head in order to close her mouth, which had been open, before the onset of rigor mortis. She was quickly put into a big, trans-parent, hermetically sealed plastic bag, zipped closed with an endlessly echoing shriek.

79

Freddy can feel illness gaining ground on him, with some kind of animal instinct. He asks me to move to Amsterdam by myself. He wants to return to his home town near Antwerp, with his sister and doctor close by. We will of course see each other often, but he wants to be alone. I leave for Amsterdam with death in my soul. I struggle to find an apartment. One night, weary of the rejection by rental agencies of the meagre guaranties I can offer, I step into a random bar for a little 'time out'. I leave a good deal later and merrier and, in the middle of the square, in the middle of the night, start screaming at the sky: 'Grandma! If there is a God, I need to find an apartment now. Now!'

I'm losing my mind. The owner of the bar comes running out and asks me what's going on. I repeat my invocation, just as intensely.

'Calm down! Calm down, lady!'

He points at a building on the corner and offers me an apartment of his, which has just become free.

'It's no film star's palace, but it's quite comfortable!'

'Thank you . . .'

I moved in the next day, thinking that I should perhaps invoke God and my grandmother more often.

80

At the end of 2001, a persistent earache changes my life. My doctor doesn't think it serious, but I am convinced.

Nothing can ease this pain that stretches from the top of my neck to my temple. A more careful examination reveals throat cancer, the scourge of smokers and alcoholics. It had sometimes crossed my mind that I couldn't emerge unscathed from my life of excess, that I would be punished or marked by it. Now it has happened – the brakes are really on now. The doctors are clear: it might all be over, but my chances of survival are very high. I get ready to age by ten years.

'Will I live to be fifty?'

'It's absolutely possible . . .'

The doctors won't take any risks. I don't want scientific statistics, I want hope. I'll hardly be suing them if they're wrong!

It's more likely that I will survive, which is just as well as I can't believe I'm going to die. I will follow the treatment meticulously and everything will be fine. Chemo and radio. I spend a while vomiting copiously, trying to kid myself that I'm hung-over. The impressive ray-producing machines remind me of science fiction. My producer friends Dorna and Ruud offer me a project, a short film that will keep me busy and entertained. Dorna wants to film me in this medical setting, in the intimacy of my illness. She says that the film may be useful to others – or serve as a post-mortem documentary, though she doesn't say that. I agree. The film makes me feel as if my illness is virtual, just another role. It gives me a bit of distance, and I feel better. Perhaps the doctors will take more care of me because they're being filmed. I am happy to be back – for the last time, perhaps – with the complicit camera.

My neck is becoming more and more wrinkled, grilled by the rays like a piece of dried fruit. One particular patch of skin is irreversibly burnt and becomes insensitive to touch: a taste of death under my scarf, an aperitif. I am defiant. I continue being cheerful, behaving as if nothing was happening. The pretty actress smiles at the camera. I no longer drink, I no longer smoke. At last.

My full, rich life may come to an end; death is so illogical.

My life is incomplete. I recover.

81

My little split-level apartment is very light, but the size of the St-Tropez kitchen. Upstairs is my bedroom, containing the only star's accessory I have left, an enormous squishy sofa.

I spend hours up there savouring my recovery, reading and watching the soaps. There's a skylight in the sloping ceiling, as there was in room 22. I have no space to paint large canvases so I reduce the size of my brushstrokes accordingly, adapting myself to more modest formats, to my smaller life.

82

One day I wake up in a new kind of discomfort. It is early 2004. The pain is in my back this time, stubborn and piercing. An invisible creature poking me from behind. I even turn round once or twice to check. My back is being poked more and more often – lying down, in the car, in the shower, all the time.

'It's nothing serious.'

That's the doctor's first diagnosis. I ask for an X-ray. They change their minds, pointing out on the backlit wall some leftover cancer – metastasis in the lungs – still troubling me two years after my remission. I now have a fist permanently pushing into the space between my shoulder blades, and my breath rasps a little. They operate, cutting out a piece of the affected lung as a matter of urgency. A few friends come by looking upset. My family, my son. Elaine flies to my bedside from Los Angeles. She feeds me tenderly with 'darling!'s, and strokes my close-cropped hair. Emmanuelle is not looking so good. I try to cheer up my visitors. I promise Elaine, who has to go, that we'll see each other again. She believes me.

'You're like a ball, darling, you bounce right back!'

Elaine is right. I recover again.

I am not afraid of death, I would just like to choose it, as my final desire.

83

Freddy dies of a heart attack in summer 2004. I am still in hospital. My sister conceals the news in an effort to protect me, then comes clean in case I hear it on TV. A few minutes later I do indeed hear them announce: 'The poet Freddy De Vree has died.'

I struggle to the funeral crammed full of painkillers. My torso is as stiff as a lump of metal. I want to be there for Freddy.

I return home and lie on my sofa for several days, alone, silent and unable to sleep. My breathing is still constrained. I take care. I have to avoid sudden movements. My mood must be calm. I am given chemical assistance, but I've built up quite a tolerance over the years and nothing manages to diminish the pain in my body. I gather my thoughts. I imagine Freddy, focus on him intensely. I still speak to him, ask him to keep watch over me, to give me some sort of sign – a light bulb blowing suddenly, a bird perching on the window ledge . . .

Wim Verstappen follows Freddy that same year.

In the end they all died. The father, the mother, the friend and the lover.

But not me.

84

I am lying languidly on the king-size bed of a luxury hotel suite, daydreaming. Outside the sky is so blue it's almost white, and great yachts are swaying on the calm sea. The palm trees are motionless and there's a dull roar coming up from the street below.

Back in Cannes. The Palais. My glitzy dress doesn't belong to me. I am bored. This break is going on too long. Suddenly, I have an idea: I'll break up the elegant uniformity of these cloth-covered walls. I don't have any paints or brushes. Oh yeah? I leap out of the bed, grab my vanity case and brandish all my reds. I take off the tops and turn up the oily, bright tips. I draw with nervous frenzy, covering each bit of cloth with lines and curves; I am tagging, gloating, disfiguring the walls, changing the set.

That scene didn't happen. I invented it. It belongs to the short film *Topor and Me*, begun with Dorna and Ruud during my illness. The film won me a prize at the Tribeca Film Festival; for directing.

It's a fictionalised autobiographical animation.

I wanted my life and art – my existence – to be discovered through painting. I suggested an animation. Some of my drawings served as a set and we wrote a shortened version of my life story. We were lacking an artistic pillar; I didn't want to shoot something that was just about me. I wanted to be accompanied in this adventure, to make an acknowledgement, a link between my life as an actress and as an artist. Choosing Hugo would have been a bit déjà vu, a bit Marilyn and Miller, too regretful. The idea of Topor was instinctive: I will pay homage to my wonderful instigator with the dirty laugh. In my film Topor represents the man as artist – carnivorous, sensual, talented, generous, enchanting. Perfect!

The film sweeps through the years from *Emmanuelle* to now in just a few minutes. It describes my hatching – the good and the good only.

I am drawn in an almost naive style; a brightly coloured doll always a little surprised, quirky, mischievous, watching the great master.

A flashback to big people and influential events. I do a voiceover in my mother tongue, my tone flat and aloof. I had remembered a play called *Dare to Live!* that I acted in five years earlier in Amsterdam. The director asked me to read the text without inflection. He said that the emotion was in my voice, not my acting. I must let it be heard, as plainly as possible.

'Don't act! Read as if your voice were naked.'

The play was a success, my talent acknowledged.

I repeated the formula and it worked again. *Topor and Me* won awards. Sometimes you have to wait a long time to feel proud of yourself.

85

From time to time my agent Monita arranges television appearances for me. A few thousand euros to talk about *Emmanuelle*. I respond to the same questions again and again, looking detached and cheerful, saying how fascinating it was to be a sex symbol, and explaining that my once debauched life is now quiet. I am a painter.

I bump into a few actor and musician friends. I saw Pierre Bachelet again a few weeks before his death. We were in make-up together. He seemed touched. I was too – an unexpected chance to turn back the years. He knew he was dying. We talked about our respective illnesses like a pair of ex-soldiers. I remember the make-up artist struggling to disguise Pierre's pallor.

More recently I appeared in a popular, modern-style French TV programme.

The presenter is humorous and saucy; young people like him, it seems. He is accompanied by a young blonde woman wearing a short lace nightie. I've been dreading crude, sensationalist questions from the presenter. But I am wrong, he is actually respectful and modest. The surprise comes from his barely dressed colleague, who asks me point-blank: 'How many . . . ?'

I don't hear the rest of the question. The sound isn't good, and her question has taken me by surprise. This woman presenter is sitting on my left and I haven't heard well on that side since chemotherapy.

I am too proud to ask her to repeat the question. We were talking about erotic scenes, faked and real, and then about my career. Naively, I think she must out of female solidarity have wanted to enlarge the debate and remind viewers of my wider filmography. So I think, 'How many . . . films?' and reply with gentle confidence:

'Oh, about fifty . . .'

The young woman is choking with laughter, and the male presenter too. In fact the whole studio is laughing their heads off. I know I can be funny sometimes, but not that funny! I've clearly chosen the wrong career, I should have been a stand-up comic. It seems I have misunderstood the question. The programme is pre-recorded so they stop the tape. 'Let's do it again!' The young woman asks for her make-up to be retouched; my friend Irene, who has come with me, takes advantage of the break to whisper the real question: 'How many orgasms?'

Now this is a surprising, delicate question, and I still don't understand it! How many orgasms? In one go? So I really am a freak show then? How many per film? In my life altogether? I don't reply, not looking so sweet any more – in fact rather annoyed – and the woman proceeds straight to the next question.

I take my cheque, ring Monita to ask if she has any other great ideas for TV appearances, and get on the train back to Amsterdam with Irene.

There is six months' rent in my bag and – now the anger has

passed – the beginning of a contagious fit of giggles on my relaxed lips. We drink beer after beer to crassness, to stupidity! It's a happy journey. Neither Irene nor I can say the word 'orgasm' without triggering off another burst of liberating laughter.

I think, *if the silly cow only knew . . .*

86

I pay regular visits to the two women who inspired and helped me, Aunt Mary and Sister Immaculata.

My aunt is still alive. She has survived electroshock therapy, social exclusion, lithium, cancer of the kidney, contempt . . . everything. 'I've buried them all!' she shouts. This crazy, useless, lost woman now lives a happy, stabilised life. Her seed of madness has germinated; my aunt is gentle, authentic, alive! Being crazy must keep you young.

For many, many years Sister Marie Immaculata remains curious, warm and funny, with perfect bearing. She still asks for my news, wanting to know everything about me, my family, my plans. Wanting me to tell her about a world she doesn't know. She waits for me, I'm a reference point, I exercise her memory and am a source of pride too, she says. She tells me that I've had a great career, and travelled a long road. Kindness keeps you young, too.

These days she's doing less well. When I last visited I thanked her again for those happy years, and her important role in my life.

I'm kind and a little crazy, so I must have some chance of growing old!

87

I love Sundays. It's an extra, bonus day.

My father loved us on Sundays.

He gave us his time as if he knew he needed to, and that one happy day in the week would make all the others worthwhile. He used to take us out, away from the hotel and the city. We would go to the countryside – in winter to the forest, where we went out hunting with him, in summer to the lake, to that water which is always close at hand in my country. Utrecht is surrounded by little islands. My father had a boat with portholes and two small cabins right at sea level. Aunt Mary often came with us. She would be singing her head off, shouting that autumn was her favourite time of year. She loved that middling season, neither too cold nor too hot, neither too bright nor too gloomy, as pleasant as a dream.

On Sundays, my father belonged to us. I would feel that childish delight at having something of my own, something alive and present, for the duration of a happy day full of loving gestures. My father knew how to imbue that day with the brightness and rhythm of his *joie de vivre*, suddenly present as if by magic. He made us laugh, and the more he drank the more we laughed. My mother too would be drinking and laughing . . .

My father puts an arm around my mother's waist and they

dance, the music playing in their heads; my mother pretends to be reluctant, then gives in with a loud, shouting laugh. My father and my mother are happy together, there, at that moment.

My father would take us out and I would go gladly, always ready to forgive. For that day I would forget his absence, the way he turned a deaf ear to us, his children, who were both the magical continuation of his life and its unbearable reflection.

My father suffered, drank, enjoyed himself and loved, on Sundays; he loved us on Sundays.

The sun glints on the lake, my mother dances alone with her shadow, intoxicated, as my father swings us around by the arms. Held in his centrifugal force we laugh and laugh, until he falls over, and night comes.

88

My son is the most precious thing in the world to me. What life has left me. He is affectionate, he understands me, loves me, tells me so, smiles at me. When I see him I see myself. He has known the men in my life, he has followed me, I have let him grow up far from the racket, far from his mother on her road to ruin.

He has accepted and forgiven everything. He is handsome, tall and straightforward. When my son is happy I'm happy too, and at those moments I tell myself that I've done well with him.

He is not ambitious. He isn't interested in money, it's a pointless quest according to him; he doesn't want to be famous because that's absurd; he says he is without talent, because 'it skips a generation!' He claims that he can't write, can't paint, can't sing, and doesn't give a damn. He works in the coffee shop of his beloved aunt Marianne, who has become rich. He lives freely, lovingly; unconstrained, with no concern for deadlines or targets.

He phones me when I'm on the road. He worries. He wants to be sure that I'm OK, and these calls from my son, who expects nothing from me, touch me to the core. I sometimes feel ashamed at having let this affectionate soul grow up so far from me. I am a late-developing, loving mother who is making up for lost time.

89

I have never belonged to anyone, and I regret it. Not to my father, nor my mother. Men have loved my body, I have been their fantasy, but I've seen few hearts. My fans were faceless, and I didn't belong to myself.

No one has taken my heart in their hand. I haven't given it. I have wandered, sought, run through life from room to room, barely awake, wild but tidy, a strange hybrid. I have lent myself, rented myself out, but never given myself. I have looked for my father and never found him. I have sought out ruin, and almost attained it. I was completely ungrounded, flying around between light and shadow. I flew, always moving, forgetting in the activity that resembles life that I belonged to no one. I wanted to be big when I was nothing but a child. I wanted to be looked at and that's all that ever happened.

I returned to my country in order to belong, return to the beginning, speak in my own language again, complete the circle, recover my senses – the hotel razed to the ground, the racket of the attic, the Underberg-scented mouths, my parents dancing in the light of the lake. To refind my life that was turning out so badly, and in refinding it, change it.

I wanted to go back in time, to see my mother and father again, to persuade them to stay around, to understand each other, to give me back the life they had both given and taken away.

Impossible, perhaps. But then 'impossible' has never meant much to me. I have achieved the impossible.

I am an ageing actress, a convalescent artist, and a woman finally stripping herself bare.